VOICES OF VIRTUE

VOICES OF VIRTUE

Inspiring Stories of Character

RANDY TRAEGER

Deep River
BOOKS

Sisters, Oregon

VOICES OF VIRTUE: INSPIRING STORIES OF CHARACTER

© 2015 by Randy Traeger

Published by Deep River Books
Sisters, Oregon
http://www.deepriverbooks.com

ISBN 13: 9781940269375

Library of Congress Control Number: 2014960368

Printed in the USA

Cover design: Jason Enterline
Interior design: Juanita Dix

CONTENTS

INTRODUCTION

Humans used stories and myths long before writing was invented. The purpose of stories was for people to deduce universal truths or virtues through observation of human behavior, in order to develop possible solutions to their own predicaments. Stories and myths have the power to reach within us, stimulate emotion, and compel involvement. Stories can help us to clarify the way we feel and fuel desire for change.

Technology is racing ahead of us at lightning speed. Yet in spite of all the excitement, the human brain appears to lag behind in its evolutionary trajectory. Our brains still respond to content by looking for a story to make sense out of an experience. No matter how fancy the style of delivery is, meaning starts in the brain.

Stories are authentic human experiences. Stories leapfrog technology and bring us to the core of experience, as any good storyteller knows. There are several psychological reasons why stories are so powerful.

- Stories have always been a primal form of communication, providing timeless links to ancient traditions, legends, archetypes, myths, and symbols.
- Stories transcend generations, engaging us through emotions and connecting us to one another. Through stories we share passions, sadness, hardships, and joys. Stories are the common ground that allow people to communicate and overcome our defenses and differences.
- Stories are a way to explain how things work, how we make decisions, how we justify our decisions, how we persuade others, how we understand our place in the world, create our identities, and define and teach virtues.
- Stories provide order. Humans seek certainty and narrative structure that is familiar, predictable, and comforting. Within the context of story, we know resolution will usually follow conflict. We can experience life with a safety net.

- Stories are how we are wired. Imagined experiences are processed in the brain, the same way real experiences are. Stories create genuine emotions, presence, and behavioral responses. Through stories, we can step out of our own shoes, see differently, and increase our empathy for others.

Think of what happens after you've watched a good movie with a friend. Not only does the story create a warm bond between us, but once it is finished, we often automatically turn to each other to talk and share our responses. When we internalize a story and begin to personify the virtues of its characters, great things can happen.

So perhaps stories are the best way to connect with young people, whose lives are being negatively impacted by today's toxic, mass-media-influenced culture. This compilation of positive tales brings together the collective voices of storytellers from across the ages to modern day. Some are true; others are quite imaginary. All are timeless. You'll find them organized conveniently as a resource to help you emphasize good character to the young folks in your life, opening doors to help them reap the rewards of a life of virtue.

CHASTITY

THE CHASTE PRINCE

This is the story about the son of a king who understood who he was and how he should act. King Louis XVI of France was taken from his throne and put in prison. His young son, the prince, was also taken by those who had captured the king. Because the young prince was to be the next king, his captors wanted to destroy him morally. They knew that if they did, he would never be able to become the king of France.

These people took the prince to a faraway city, where they tempted the boy with every filthy thing they could find. They tried to get him to eat foods that would quickly make him lose control of himself. They used terrible language around him all the time. They tempted him with evil women. They exposed him to dishonor and distrust. They surrounded him constantly by everything that could make a person lose his moral values. For more than six months he was given this treatment, but not once did the boy give in to temptation. Finally, after doing everything they could think of, they asked him why he did not participate in the temptations. The prince replied, "I cannot do what you ask, for I was born to be a king."

We too were born to be kings, and as such, we must respect ourselves, respect the opposite sex, and respect humanity. We do so by practicing the virtue of chastity and clinging to our moral standards.

ENTHUSIASM

CHARLES SCHWAB

Many decades ago, Charles Schwab, who was earning a salary of a million dollars a year, was asked if he was paid such a high salary because of his exceptional ability to produce steel. Schwab replied, "I consider my ability to arouse enthusiasm among the men the greatest asset I possess, and the way to develop the best that is in a man is by appreciation and encouragement."[1]

Live while you are alive. Don't die before you are dead. Enthusiasm and desire are what change mediocrity to excellence.

Water turns into steam with a difference of only one degree in temperature, and steam can move some of the biggest engines in the world. That is what enthusiasm helps us do in our lives.

THE GREATEST SALESMAN IN THE WORLD

Arthur "Red" Motley was a master salesman and a prolific motivational speaker and writer who spent fifty years in the publishing profession. In 1958 he was famously dubbed "the greatest salesman God has ever created" after he took the loss-making American magazine and turned it into a money-spinner with a weekly circulation of more than twenty million copies. Motley attributed his success to a life-changing experience he had while a university student. To earn extra money he sold musical instruments, and he was very successful at it. One day he accidentally discovered that his instruments were faulty in that they produced a discordant C note. Although he never received a single complaint from his customers, who continued to extol the virtues of his instruments, from the day he made the discovery his sales plummeted. He had lost belief in his product and his mission.[2]

The moment you lose faith in your mission and product is the moment your enthusiasm begins to die and your chances of success diminish.

THE BURNING DESIRE

A young man asked Socrates the secret to success. Socrates told the young man to meet him near the river the next morning. They met. Socrates asked the young man to walk with him toward the river. When the water got up to their necks, Socrates took the young man by surprise and ducked him into the water. The boy struggled to get out, but Socrates was strong and kept him there until the boy started turning blue. Socrates pulled his head out of the water, and the first thing the young man did was gasp and take a deep breath of air. Socrates asked, "What did you want the most when you were there?" The boy replied, "Air." Socrates said, "That is the secret to success. When you want success as badly as you wanted the air, then you will get it." There is no other secret.

COUNSEL

WHO PACKED YOUR PARACHUTE?

Sometimes in the daily challenges that life gives us, we miss what is most important. We may fail to say hello, please, or thank you, congratulate someone on something wonderful that has happened to them, give a compliment, or just do something nice for no reason.

Charles Plumb, a US Naval Academy graduate, was a jet pilot in Vietnam. After seventy-five combat missions, his plane was destroyed by a surface-to-air missile. Plumb ejected and parachuted into enemy lands. He was captured and spent six years in a communist Vietnamese prison. He survived the ordeal and now lectures on lessons learned from that experience.

One day, when Plumb and his wife were sitting in a restaurant, a man at another table approached and said, "You're Plumb! You flew jet fighters in Vietnam from the aircraft carrier Kitty Hawk. You were shot down!"

"How in the world did you know that?" Plumb asked.

"I packed your parachute," the man replied.

Plumb gasped in surprise and gratitude. The man pumped his hand, saying, "I guess it worked!"

Plumb assured him, "It sure did. If your chute hadn't worked, I wouldn't be here today."

Plumb couldn't sleep that night, thinking about that man. Plumb says, "I kept wondering what he might have looked like in a Navy uniform: A white hat, a bib in the back, and bell bottom trousers. I wonder how many times I might have seen him and not even said good morning, how are you or anything else because, you see, I was a fighter pilot, and he was just a sailor."

Plumb thought of the many hours the sailor had spent at a long wooden table in the bowels of the ship, carefully weaving the shrouds and folding the silks of each chute, holding in his hands each time the fate of someone he didn't know.

Now, Plumb asks his audience, "Who's packing your parachute?"[1]

Everyone has someone who provides what he or she needs to make it through the day. Plumb also points out that he needed many kinds of parachutes when his plane was shot down over enemy territory. He needed his physical parachute, his mental parachute, his emotional parachute, and his spiritual parachute. He called on all these supports before reaching safety. His experience reminds us all to prepare ourselves to weather whatever storms lie ahead. As you go through this week, this month, this year, recognize the people who pack your parachute!

THE WISE OWL'S COUNSEL

A large group of owls came to settle in a jungle. The jungle was full of green and lively trees. They were free to pick a tree of their choice to build their homes.

The young owls chose a green and well-built tree for themselves. There was an old owl in their group, who was forced by the others to choose an old and half-dead tree. The old owl had to remain satisfied with his share. Days went by. The young owls would often feel proud at their selection of trees and would tease the old owl, "Oh, you poor guy! You could not find a lively and green tree. You have a dry and half-dead tree. You are very unlucky indeed." But the old owl was wise. He would silently smile at their remarks. At times he would reply, "Who knows whether you are lucky or I am lucky!" But the young owls would merely laugh at him.

One day, a large number of woodcutters came to the jungle in search of wood. The lively and green trees fascinated them. So they started felling them with their sharp axes. The young owls all started making a loud noise when they saw their homes being destroyed. They could do nothing but watch helplessly. When the woodcutters looked at the old and half-dead tree, they said, "Oh! This is a dry tree. It is of no use to us, as it won't provide us enough wood. Why waste our time on it?" They went away, leaving the old and half-dead tree untouched. The old owl's nest was spared.

ENTERPRISE

HERCULES AND THE WAGONER
AESOP

Some people exhibit an almost miraculous resolve in waiting for someone else to come along and do their work for them. This old fable may help us learn early that the only certain labor is your own.

A wagoner was driving his team along a muddy lane with a fully-loaded wagon, when the wheels sank so deep in the mire that no efforts of his horses could move them. As he stood there, looking helplessly on, and calling loudly at intervals upon Hercules for assistance, the god himself appeared and said to him, "Put your shoulder to the wheel, man, and goad on your horses, and then you may call on Hercules to assist you. If you won't lift a finger to help yourself, you can't expect Hercules or anyone else to come to your aid." Heaven helps those who help themselves.

THE FARMER AND HIS SONS

A farmer, being at death's door and desiring to impart to his sons a secret of much moment, called them round him and said, "My sons, I am shortly about to die. I would have you know that in my vineyard there lies a hidden treasure. Dig and you will find it." As soon as their father was dead, the sons took spades and forks and turned up the soil of the vineyard over and over again in their search for the treasure that they supposed lay buried there. They found none, but the vines, after so thorough a digging, produced a crop such as had never before been seen. There is no treasure without toil.

THE PARABLE OF THE PENCIL

The pencil maker took the pencil aside, just before putting him into the box.

"There are five things you need to know before I send you out into the world," he told the pencil. Always remember them and never forget, and you will become the best pencil you can be."

One: "You will be able to do many great things, but only if you allow yourself to be held in someone's hand."

Two: "You will experience a painful sharpening from time to time, but you'll need it to become a better pencil."

Three: "You will be able to correct any mistakes you might make."

Four: "The most important part of you will always be what's inside."

Five: "On every surface you are used on, you must leave your mark. No matter what the condition, you must continue to write."

The pencil understood and promised to remember, and went into the box with purpose in its heart.

Now replacing the pencil with "you," remember these five things and never forget them, and you will become the best person you can be.

One: "You will be able to do many great things, but only if you allow yourself to be held in God's hand. Allow other human beings to access you for the many gifts you possess."

Two: "You will experience a painful sharpening from time to time, by going through various problems in life, but you'll need it to become a stronger person."

Three: "You will be able to correct any mistakes you might make."

Four: "The most important part of you will always be what's on the inside."

Five: "On every surface you walk through, you must leave your mark. No matter what the situation, you must continue to do your duties."

SINCERITY

THE RUBYLAND

In the palace of Rubyland there was a ruby thief. No one knew who it was, and the thief had everyone so fooled that the only thing known about him was that he lived in the palace, and that when you were in the palace you should always hide your jewels.

The King decided to find out who it was, and he asked for help from a wise dwarf who was famed for his intelligence. The dwarf spent some days there, watching and listening until there was another theft. The following morning the wise dwarf made all the palace inhabitants meet together in the same room. After inspecting them for the entire morning and during lunch without saying a word, the dwarf started asking them all, one by one, what they knew about the stolen jewels.

Once again, it seemed that no one had been the thief. Then, suddenly, one of the gardeners began coughing, writhing, and moaning, and finally he fell to the floor.

The dwarf, with a cheeky smile, explained that the food they had just eaten was poisoned, and the only antidote for this poison was hidden inside the ruby that had been stolen the previous night. He explained how, some days earlier, he had swapped some false rubies for the genuine ones. He expected that only the thief would be able to save the gardener's life, since the poison was particularly quick acting. The coughs and groans spread around the room, and terror took hold of all present—all except one person. A footman quickly ran to where he had hidden the jewels and took out the ruby. Fortunately, he was able to open it and drink the strange liquid inside, thus saving his life—or so he believed. The gardener was, in fact, one of the dwarf's assistants, and the poison was nothing more than a potion prepared by the little investigator to cause a few strong pains for

9

a short while, but nothing more than that. The footman, now found out, was arrested by the guards and taken immediately to court.

The grateful king generously rewarded his wise adviser. When he asked the dwarf what his secret was, the dwarf smiled and said, "I try to get the person who knows the truth to reveal that truth."

"And who knew it? What if the thief had deceived everyone?" said the king.

"No, your majesty, not everyone," replied the wise advisor. "Anyone can deceive everyone, but no one can deceive himself."

THE BOY WHO CRIED WOLF
AESOP

There once was a shepherd boy who was bored as he sat on the hillside watching the village sheep. To amuse himself, he took a great breath and sang out, "Wolf! Wolf! The Wolf is chasing the sheep!"

The villagers came running up the hill to help the boy drive the wolf away. When they arrived at the top of the hill, they found no wolf. The boy laughed at the sight of their angry faces.

"Don't cry 'wolf,' shepherd boy," said the villagers, "when there's no wolf!" They went grumbling back down the hill.

Later, the boy sang out again, "Wolf! Wolf! The wolf is chasing the sheep!" To his naughty delight, he watched the villagers run up the hill to help him drive the wolf away.

When the villagers saw no wolf, they sternly said, "Save your frightened song for when there is really something wrong! Don't cry 'wolf' when there is NO wolf!"

The boy just grinned and watched them go grumbling down the hill once more.

Later, he saw a real wolf prowling about his flock. Alarmed, he leaped to his feet and sang out as loudly as he could, "Wolf! Wolf!"

The villagers thought he was trying to fool them again, and so they didn't come.

At sunset, everyone wondered why the shepherd boy hadn't returned to the village with their sheep. They went up the hill to find the boy. They found him weeping.

"There really was a wolf here! The flock has scattered! I cried out, 'Wolf!' Why didn't you come?"

An old man tried to comfort the boy as they walked back to the village.

"We'll help you look for the lost sheep in the morning," he said, putting his arm around the youth. "Nobody believes a liar...even when he is telling the truth!"

FRIENDLINESS

What is real endures; it is as true of friendship as of other kinds of love.

NEW AND OLD FRIENDS
JOSEPH PARRY

Make new friends, but keep the old; those are silver, these are gold.
New-made friendships, like new wine, Age will mellow and refine.
Friendships that have stood the test, time and change are surely best.
Brow may wrinkle, hair grow gray; Friendship never knows decay.
For 'mid old friends, tried and true, Once more we our youth renew.
But old friends, alas, may die; new friends must their place supply.
Cherish friendship in your breast. New is good, but old is best.
Make new friends, but keep the old; those are silver, these are gold.[1]

THE HARE WITH TOO MANY FRIENDS
AESOP

A hare was very popular with the other animals in the jungle who all claimed to be her friends. One day she heard the hounds approaching and she hoped to escape them with the aid of her friends. She went to the horse and asked him to carry her away from the hounds. He declined, stating that he had important work to do for his master. He felt sure, he said, that all her other friends would come to her assistance. She then applied to the bull, and hoped that he would repel the hounds with his horns. The bull replied, "I am very sorry, but I have an appointment with a lady; but I feel sure that our friend the goat will do what you want." The goat, however, feared that his back might do her some harm if he took her upon it. The ram, he felt sure, was the proper friend to ask for help. She went to the ram and told him the case. The ram replied, "Another time, my dear friend. I do not like to interfere on the present occasion, as hounds have been known to eat sheep as well as hares." The hare then applied, as a last hope, to the calf, who regretted that he was unable to help her, as he did not like to take the responsibility upon himself, as so many older persons than himself had declined the task. By this time, the hounds were quite near, and the hare took to her heels and luckily escaped. The moral of the story is that he who has many friends, has no friends.

SOCRATES' FRIENDS

In ancient Greece, Socrates was reputed to hold knowledge in high esteem. One day a fellow met the great philosopher and said, "Do you know what I just heard about your friend?"

"Hold on a minute," Socrates replied. "Before telling me anything, I'd like you to pass a little test. It's called the Triple Filter Test."

"Triple filter?"

"That's right," Socrates continued. "Before you talk to me about my friend, it might be a good idea to take a moment and filter what you're going to say. That's why I call it the triple filter test. The first filter is Truth. Have you made absolutely sure that what you are about to tell me is true?"

"No," the man said, "actually I just heard about it and…"

"All right," said Socrates. "So you don't know if it's true or not. Now let's try the second filter, the filter of goodness. Is what you are about to tell me about my friend something good?"

"No, on the contrary…"

"So," Socrates continued, "you want to tell me something bad about him, but you're not certain it's true. You may still pass the test though, because there's one filter left: the filter of usefulness. Is what you want to tell me about my friend going to be useful to me?"

"No, not really."

"Well," concluded Socrates, "if what you want to tell me is neither true nor good nor even useful, why tell it to me at all?"

We can always participate in loose talk to curb our boredom. But when it comes to your friends, it's not worth it. Always avoid talking behind the backs of your near and dear friends.

GENTLENESS

THE NORTH WIND AND THE SUN
AESOP

The North Wind boasted of great strength. The Sun argued that there was great power in gentleness. "We shall have a contest," said the Sun. Far below, a man traveled a winding road. He was wearing a warm winter coat.

"As a test of strength," said the Sun, "Let us see which of us can take the coat off of that man."

"It will be quite simple for me to force him to remove his coat," bragged the Wind.

The Wind blew so hard, the birds clung to the trees. The world was filled with dust and leaves. But the harder the Wind blew down the road, the tighter the shivering man clung to his coat.

Then, the Sun came out from behind a cloud. The Sun warmed the air and the frosty ground. The man on the road unbuttoned his coat.

The sun grew slowly brighter and brighter. Soon the man felt so hot, he took off his coat and sat down in a shady spot. "How did you do that?" said the Wind.

"It was easy," said the Sun, "I lit the day. Through gentleness I got my way."

THE GOLD FISH
RICHARD L. DUNAGIN

At their school carnival, our kids won four free goldfish (lucky us!), so out I went Saturday morning to find an aquarium. The first few I priced ranged from $40 to $70. Then I spotted it—right in the aisle: a discarded 10-gallon display tank, complete with gravel and filter for a mere five bucks. Sold! Of course it was nasty dirty, but the savings made the two hours of clean up a breeze.

Those four new fish looked great in their new home, at least for the first day. By Sunday one had died. Too bad, but three remained. Monday morning revealed a second casualty, and by Monday night a third gold-fish had gone belly up. We called in an expert, a member of our church who has a thirty-gallon tank. It didn't take him long to discover the prob-lem: I had washed the tank with soap, an absolute no-no. My uninformed efforts had destroyed the very lives I was trying to protect. Sometimes in our zeal to clean up our own lives or the lives of others, we unfortunately use "killer soaps": condemnation, criticism, nagging, fits of temper. We think we're doing right, but our harsh, self-righteous treatment is more than they can bear. We need to be gentle with people.[1]

HONOR

THE LAKOTA INDIANS
JOSEPH MARSHALL

The Lakota tribe was known to have some of the greatest warriors of all time. They were feared in battle. Every young man was raised to be a warrior for the tribe. Within the tribe of warriors was a small group of men called the Red Shirt Warriors. The color red in Lakota culture stood for honor. They were the best of the best, a prestigious club that every young warrior wanted to strive to be a part of.

Every four years, the Red Shirt Warriors extended an invitation to a select few of the young warriors to test themselves in order to be admitted to the group. The physical tests were difficult and not all those invited were able to pass. The first tests were ones that allowed the young warriors to demonstrate the skills of battle: marksmanship, horsemanship, etc. The last test given to the elite group was a difficult test of endurance.

The test had a time limit of four days and was done during the hottest part of the year. Each young warrior was sent out alone, without food or water and only a knife for protection. He was told to follow a well-known path to a high shale cliff. Warriors were instructed to climb the high cliff and recover a red sash that had been tied to a stone at the top of the mountain. Their goal was to recover the sash from the top of the cliff and return to camp with it within the four-day time period. Little did they know that the tribal elders had actually placed two red sashes on the mountain. One rolled up tied red sash that when unfurled was about 6 feet long had been placed at the top of the mountain on the high cliff (which is the one they were instructed to retrieve), and one rolled up tied red sash that when unfurled was only about three-feet long which had been placed at the bottom of the mountain just off the side of the trail and easily gotten. Because of the difficulty and distance, the young warriors would usually get back by sunset of the fourth day, exhausted, thirsty, and hungry. Upon arriving back to the tribe and before they were given any food or water, they were escorted into the lodge of the Red Shirt Warriors and asked to present the sash they had recovered.

According to the stories, no one tested ever returned without a red sash. The sash was held tightly in their hands. Each young man was asked to hold one end of the sash at head height and let it unfurl toward the ground. If it extended all the way to the ground, the man had gained membership as a Red Shirt Warrior. If it did not reach the ground, he was denied membership and was never allowed another opportunity to join the elite group. No explanation was given to the ones denied and no explanation was ever needed, because it wasn't just a test of endurance, but more importantly, a test of honor.[1]

HONORING OUR ELDERLY

Once there was a little old man. His eyes blinked and his hands trembled. When he ate, he clattered the silverware distressingly, missed his mouth with the spoon as often as not, and dribbled a bit of his food on the tablecloth. Now he lived with his married son, having nowhere else to live, but his son's wife didn't like the arrangement.

"I can't have this," she said. "It interferes with my right to happiness." So she and her husband took the old man gently but firmly by the arm and led him to the corner of the kitchen. There they sat him on a stool and gave him his food in an earthenware bowl. From then on, he always ate in the corner, blinking at the table with wistful eyes. One day his hands trembled rather more than usual, and the earthenware bowl fell and broke.

"If you are a pig," said the daughter-in-law, "you must eat out of a trough." So they made him a little wooden trough and he got his meals in that.

These people had a four-year-old son of whom they were very fond. One evening the young man noticed his boy playing intently with some bits of wood and asked what he was doing.

"I'm making a trough," he said, smiling up for approval, "to feed you and Mamma out of when I get big."

The man and his wife looked at each other for a while and didn't say anything. Then they cried a little. They then went to the corner, took the old man by the arm, and led him back to the table. They sat him in a comfortable chair and gave him his food on a plate, and from then on, nobody ever scolded when he clattered or spilled or broke things.

HENRY THE EIGHTH AND SIR THOMAS MORE

Henry the Eighth, King of England, had a bad habit of getting rid of an existing wife to replace her with a new one. At the time, Christendom was Catholic and the Pope was the leader of the faithful. Because the Pope would not approve King Henry's actions, King Henry set himself up as head of the church in England. Everyone in England simply adjusted their religious beliefs to accommodate the king except for Sir Thomas More.

Sir Thomas More was a wealthy and well-respected figure in England, and the King had made him Lord Chancellor over the chancery courts, the "courts of the King's conscience," which could administer equitable relief to correct wrongs. Sir Thomas More was a man of irreproachable character, who could not be bribed or bullied into abusing the power of his position. As it happens, that same quality of character prevented him from signing a document supporting the King's action in essentially declaring the Pope irrelevant to England. Sir Thomas More did not publically oppose the King, but he refused to sign the document, and the King found it intolerable that one of the most respected and honorable men in the country apparently privately questioned the King's actions.

Ultimately, a royal flunky staged a trial at which it became clear that Sir Thomas More must either submit or lose his head. Sir Thomas More grieved to cause King Henry difficulty, but as loyal as he wanted to be to the king, he owed his loyalty first to God. Since More believed the Pope to be God's chosen servant, he could not accept the king's supremacy in matters of religion. Death was sure, but since death comes to us all, and what matters is not how we die, but how we live, Sir Thomas More stood true to his conscience even as the axe fell.

HUMOR

THE LIFE SENTENCE

A woman awoke during the night to find that her husband was not in bed. She put on her robe and went downstairs to look for him. She found him sitting in the kitchen with a cup of coffee, and he appeared to be in deep thought, just staring at the wall. She watched as he wiped a tear from his eye and took a sip of coffee.

"What's the matter, dear?" she whispered as she stepped into the room. "Why are you sitting down here this time of the night?"

The husband looked up from his coffee. "Do you remember twenty years ago when we were dating, and you were only sixteen?" he asked, solemnly.

"Yes, I do," she replied.

The husband paused; the words were not coming easily. "Do you remember when your father caught us in the back seat of my car making love?"

"Yes. I remember," the wife said, lowering herself into a chair beside him.

The husband continued. "Do you remember when he shoved the double-barrel shotgun in my face and said, 'Either you marry my daughter, or I'll send you to jail for twenty years'?"

"Yes, I remember that too," she whispered softly.

He wiped another tear from his cheek. "I would be getting out of prison today!"

A BEAUTY

A couple came by a Baptist parsonage on Saturday afternoon and asked if the pastor would marry them. The bride was wearing a veil and the pastor could not see her face. Following the ceremony, the groom said, "Preacher, how much do I owe you?"

"There is no charge," the pastor replied.

"But I want to show my appreciation," the groom said, and he gave him five dollars.

At this point, the bride took off her veil, and the minister, seeing her face, gave the groom three dollars in change.

LAUGHTER CURES

Norman Cousins, philosopher and speaker, had developed a life-threatening disease for which there was no known cure. Cousins checked out of the hospital and into a cheerful environment in a hotel. He began to watch funny movies, especially old *Candid Camera* programs. He found that one ten-minute period of laughter gave him two hours of pain-less sleep. Ten years later, by changing his dietary habits and laughing as long and as often as he wanted, he was functioning at a maximum level, reversing all previous medical predictions.[1]

SELF-DISCIPLINE

Brave men and women (as well as cowardly men and women) are not born that way; they become that way through their acts. Here are the acts that make us not just grow up, but grow up well.

IF
RUDYARD KIPLING

If you can keep your head when all about you
Are losing theirs and blaming it on you;
If you can trust yourself when all men doubt you,
But make allowance for their doubting too:
If you can wait and not be tired by waiting,
Or being lied about, don't deal in lies,
Or being hated, don't give way to hating,
And yet don't look too good, nor talk too wise;

If you can dream—and not make dreams your master;
If you can think—and not make thoughts your aim,
If you can meet with Triumph and Disaster
And treat those two impostors just the same:
If you can bear to hear the truth you've spoken
Twisted by knaves to make a trap for fools,
Or watch the things you gave your life to, broken,
And stoop and build 'em up with worn-out tools;

If you can make one heap of all your winnings
And risk it on one turn of pitch-and-toss,
And lose, and start again at your beginnings

And never breathe a word about your loss:
If you can force your heart and nerve and sinew
To serve your turn long after they are gone,
And so hold on when there is nothing in you
Except the Will which says to them: "Hold on!"

If you can talk with crowds and keep your virtue,
Or walk with Kings—nor lose the common touch,
If neither foes nor loving friends can hurt you,
If all men count with you, but none too much:
If you can fill the unforgiving minute
With sixty seconds' worth of distance run,
Yours is the Earth and everything that's in it,
And—which is more—you'll be a Man, my son!

THE BOY AND THE NAILS

There once was a little boy who had a bad temper. His father gave
him a bag of nails and told him that every time he lost his temper, he
must hammer a nail into the back of the fence. The first day, the boy had
driven thirty-seven nails into the fence. Over the next few weeks, as he
learned to control his anger, the number of nails hammered daily gradually dwindled down. He discovered it was easier to hold his temper than
to drive those nails into the fence. Finally, the day came when the boy
didn't lose his temper at all. He told his father about it and the father
suggested that the boy now pull out one nail for each day that he was able
to hold his temper. The days passed and the boy was finally able to tell
his father that all the nails were gone. The father took his son by the hand
and led him to the fence. He said, "You have done well, my son, but look
at the holes in the fence. The fence will never be the same. When you say
things in anger, they leave scars just like these. You can put a knife in a
man and draw it out. It won't matter how many times you say, 'I'm sorry;'
the wound is still there."

We need to be careful with the words we use in anger as they often
leave scars that never heal.

LEARN SELF-DISCIPLINE

An ancient Indian sage was teaching his disciples the art of archery. He put a wooden bird as the target and asked them to aim at the eye of the bird. He asked the first disciple to describe what he saw. He said, "I see the trees, the branches, the leaves, the sky, the bird and its eye." The sage asked this disciple to wait. Then he asked the second disciple the same question and he replied, "I only see the eye of the bird." The sage said, "Very good, then shoot." The arrow went straight and hit the eye of the bird.

What is the moral of the story? Unless we focus, we cannot achieve our goal. It is hard to focus and concentrate, but it is a skill that we can learn.

IT TAKES MORE THAN ENTHUSIASM TO WIN

One fall, in the panhandle of Texas, a local high school football team was enduring a terribly embarrassing season. Week after week, the hometown would show up and cheer to no avail; it was abysmal. Finally, a wealthy oilman could take it no longer. The week before the homecoming game against their archrivals, he asked to address the team. "Boys," he began, "when I wore the green and gold, we won nearly every single game. Now look at you. You've become a joke! You need some motivation. So here's my proposition. You win this one game, and I will personally buy each of you a brand new pickup truck." Those student-athletes began to think and dream about how fine they would look driving around in their new trucks. They obsessed over which girls would ride in them and what colors and accessories they would put on their new pickup trucks. They were excited about the prospect of driving a truck with that "new car" smell. They hung a big poster of a truck in the locker room and all patted the poster on their way out to take the field on game night…and they went out and lost the game thirty-eight to zero.

Enthusiasm does not make up for preparation. Exuberance doesn't translate into a single point on the scoreboard. Seven days of hurrah and whoop-de-do will never compensate for a lack of discipline, conditioning, practice, coaching, experience, and character. Those things are what will sustain you, whether it's in the locker room or the work place. We need more than good intentions. We need self-discipline. Our emotions can often reveal a vision to us. But we must develop a plan—a strategy—for accomplishing that vision, and then we must possess the self-discipline to follow through on that vision and plan. Vision, plan, and self-discipline... these are the keys to living the life of a champion.

OBEDIENCE

THE OBEDIENT KID

In a stable lived a goat that had a pretty little kid of which she was very fond. This kid was too young to go about with her mother, and the mother was afraid to leave her by herself. But the mother goat was obliged to go out to get food.

One day she said to her little kid, "My dear, I am going to fetch a cabbage and a lettuce for your dinner. Mind you do not go out while I am away. Lock the door of our stable, and do not open it to anyone who knocks without first looking out of the window to see who it is. Pray, mind what I say to you, and do as I bid you."

"Yes, Mother," said the kid. "Do not be afraid, I will do as you bid me."

So off the old goat went, but she waited outside the door while the kid shut it. She looked back often to see that it was shut.

A wolf that lived nearby saw the goat pass. He had often wished to eat up that nice, tender young kid, and on this day, having had no breakfast, he was very hungry. "Ah! Ah! Now the old mother is out, I will go and eat that silly young kid. She will be sure to leave the door open." Away he ran to the stable where the goat lived. He went to the door with a bounce, thinking to push it open. He did not expect to find the door fastened; yet he was mistaken, and he could not get in.

"Although you have fastened the door, Miss Kid," growled he to himself, "I will eat you—I will knock, and you will be sure to come and open the door. And then..." He was so pleased with the thought of eating the little goat that he licked his lips. Lifting up his paw, he gave a loud knock at the door.

"Who is there?" asked the kid from within.

"I, my dear," said the wolf, trying to speak like the goat, "I, your mother. Open the door quickly; I am in a hurry."

"Oh, no! You cannot be my mother," said the kid.

"Open the door this minute, or I shall be very angry with you," said the wolf.

"If you are my mother," said the little kid, "you will wait while I look out of the window, for my mother told me to do so before I open the door."

"Open the door directly," called out the wolf.

But the wise little kid went to the window and looked out. "Oh you are a bad wolf," said she, "to try to cheat me. You will not eat me today, so you may go away! Ha! Ha! Ha!" And the kid laughed. "I take care to mind what my dear mother says to me. Ha! Ha! Ha! Master Wolf you may go away. Ha! Ha! Ha!"

The wolf gnashed his teeth and growled. He looked fiercely at the little kid, but he could not reach her. The kid went from the window, but the wolf still heard her "Ha! Ha! Ha!" as she laughed from her place of safety inside the stable.

The wolf went away. Soon after, the mother goat came back. She knocked at the door. The little kid asked, "Who is there?"

"It is I, your mother, darling," said the goat.

"You speak like my mother, but I must be sure before I open the door. If you are my mother, you will not mind waiting while I look out of the window."

So again the kid looked out of the window, and when she saw it was her own mother, she ran quickly and opened the door.

"Dear Mother," said she, "such a large, cruel wolf has been here. But I did as you bade me; I looked out of the window before I opened the door."

"Dear kid," said the goat, and she licked the kid with her tongue. "Good kid, wise little kid. If you had not obeyed me, that cruel, greedy wolf would have eaten you up, and you would never have seen your mother again. Good child, to do as I bade you."

Then the mother goat gave her kid the fine lettuce and cabbage she had brought home with her.

OBEDIENT AS A DOG?

How we admire the obedience a dog shows to its master! Archibald Rutledge wrote that one day he met a man whose dog had just been killed in a forest fire. Heartbroken, the man explained to Rutledge how it happened. Because he worked outdoors, he often took his dog with him. That morning he left the animal in a clearing and gave him a command to stay and watch his lunch bucket while he went into the forest. His faithful friend understood, and that's exactly what he did. Then a fire started in the woods, and soon the blaze spread to the spot where the dog was. He didn't move. He stayed right where he was, in perfect obedience to his master's word. With tearful eyes, the dog's owner said, "I always had to be careful what I told him to do, because I knew he would do it."[1]

ARABIAN HORSES

Arabian horses go through rigorous training in the deserts of the Middle East. The trainers require absolute obedience from the horses. They test them to see if they are completely trained. The final test is almost beyond the endurance of any living thing. The trainers force the horses to go without water for many days. Then they turn the horses loose. Of course, they start running toward the water, but just as they get to the edge, ready to plunge in and drink, the trainer blows his whistle. The horses that have been completely trained and that have learned perfect obedience stop immediately. They turn around and come prancing back to the trainer. They stand there quivering, wanting water, but they wait in perfect obedience. When the trainer is sure that he has their obedience, he gives them a signal to go back and drink.

Now this may be severe, but when you are on the trackless desert of Arabia and your life is entrusted to a horse, you had better have a trained obedient horse. There are many times and places in our lives where we need to practice this type of obedience.

OBEDIENT EMPLOYEES

Imagine if you will that you work for a company whose president finds it necessary to travel out of the country and spend extended periods of time abroad. He says to you and the other trusted employees, "Look, I'm going to leave. While I'm gone, I want you to pay close attention to the business. You manage things while I'm away. I will write you regularly.

When I do, I will instruct you in what you should do from now until I return from this trip." Everyone agrees.

He leaves and is gone for a couple of years. During that time, he writes often, communicating his desires and concerns. Finally, he returns. He walks up to the front door of the company and immediately discovers everything is a mess—weeds flourishing in the flower beds, windows broken across the front of the building, the woman at the front desk is dozing, loud music roars from several offices, two or three people are engaging in horseplay in the back room. Instead of making a profit, the business has suffered a great loss. Without hesitation, he calls everyone together and with a frown asks, "What happened? Didn't you get my letters?"

"Oh, yeah, sure. We got all your letters. We've even bound them in a book. Some of us have memorized them. In fact, we have 'letter study' every Sunday. You know, those were really great letters." The president would ask, "What did you do about my instructions?" No doubt the employees would respond, "Do? Well...nothing. But we read every one!"

MORALITY

COACH WOODEN

When evaluating people, they say good character trumps all. Coach John Wooden always taught that character was more important than reputation because "character is what you really are, while reputation is merely what others think you are." Folks with good character never shy away from making hard decisions whenever hard decisions are necessary, and—more importantly—they always take into account the effect their actions will have on others. The bottom line: Everything we do and say in life represents a choice, and people of good moral character always strive to do the right thing—even when nobody else is paying attention.

SELF-CONTROL

MEANINGLESS GOALS

A farmer had a dog that used to sit by the roadside waiting for vehicles to pass. As soon as one came, he would run down the road, barking and trying to overtake it. One day a neighbor asked the farmer, "Do you think your dog is ever going to catch a car?" The farmer replied, "That's not what bothers me. What bothers me is what he would do if he ever caught one." Many people in life behave like that dog. They pursue meaningless goals.

MONKEY BUSINESS

A monkey climbed on the roof of a house and entertained the people who had gathered below to watch it, with its antics. After it had gone, an ass who craved popularity climbed to the roof and tried to perform the same tricks. In the process, the ass dislodged and broke several tiles. The owner of the house was furious. His servants went up, drove the ass down, and beat it black and blue.

Moral: Actions that suit others may not suit you. Be yourself.

SPOKEN WORDS CAN'T BE RETRIEVED

A farmer insulted his neighbor. Realizing his mistake, he went to the preacher to ask for forgiveness. The preacher told him to take a bag of feathers and drop them in the center of town. The farmer did as he was told. Then the preacher asked him to go and collect the feathers and put them back in the bag. The farmer tried but couldn't as the feathers had blown away. When he returned with the empty bag, the preacher said, "The same thing is true about your words. You dropped them rather easily but you cannot retrieve them, so be very careful in choosing your words."

SERVITUDE

ELIAS
LEO TOLSTOY

Leo Tolstoy told the story of a man named Elias who worked hard his whole life to amass riches and a good life, only to find that in old age he lost it all and ended up living the life of a servant.

Elias' wife narrates the story:

"For a half century we sought happiness, and as long as we were rich we never found it. Now that we have nothing left, and have taken service as laborers, we have found such happiness that we want nothing better.

"When we were rich, my husband and I had so many cares that we had no time to talk to one another or to think of our souls or to pray to God. Now we had visitors, and had to consider what food to set before them, and what presents to give them, lest they should speak ill of us. When they left, we had to look after our laborers, who were always trying to shirk work and get the best food, while we wanted to get all we could out of them. So we sinned.

"Then we were in fear lest a wolf should kill a foal or a calf, or thieves steal our horses. We lay awake at night worrying lest the ewes should overlie their lambs, and we got up again and again to see that all was well. One thing attended to, another care would spring up, such as how to get enough fodder for the winter. Besides that, my husband and I used to disagree. He would say we must do so and so, and I would differ from him; and then we disputed—sinning again.

"So we passed from one trouble to another, from one sin to another and found no happiness.

"Now, when my husband and I wake in the morning, we always have a loving word for one another, and we live peacefully having nothing to quarrel about. We have no care but how best to serve our master. We work as much as our strength allows, and do it with a will, so that our master may not lose, but profit by us. When we come in, dinner or supper is ready and there is plenty to drink. We have fuel to burn when it is cold, and we have our fur cloak. We have time to talk; time to think of our souls, and time to pray. For fifty years we sought happiness, but only now, as servants, we found it at last."[1]

FATIGUES TO FULL DRESS

There was a first-year cadet at West Point who learned that you can accomplish just about anything when you have real friends upon whom you can truly depend. There were about thirty plebes, first year cadets, in his particular platoon. They were divided three to a room. One day when they were all lined up in front of their dorm in their fatigues, an upperclassman barked out an order, "You are all to be back here in full dress uniform in exactly two minutes. Go." Now, it was pretty much considered physically impossible to run to your room, change from fatigues to full dress, leave your room in order, and run back to the line in just two minutes. But they tried. One guy finished first and away he went, then the next, and finally the third guy. They were all late and so they had to get in the late line. An officer approached them and asked, "Why are you late?"

"No excuse, sir."

"That's right, there's no excuse" But then the more important questions got fired at them. "Why aren't you out here with your roommates all together? Now listen up. If one of you is late—then all of you are late. It's not about you getting here on time; it's about the three of you getting here on time all together as a team. If you work very hard, you might make it. Learn to help one another."

Eventually the cadets learned how to do it. At first they thought it was physically impossible, but once they learned how to work together and help one another, they got it.

'The first time we all made it on time together, man did that feel good. Individually, it felt good. But as a team, as a collective unit, it felt great! We all went back to our room giving each other high fives."

THE BUNDLE OF STICKS
AESOP

A certain man had several sons who were always quarreling with one another, and try as he might, he could not get them to live together in harmony. He determined to convince them of their folly by the following means. Bidding them to fetch a bundle of sticks, he invited each in turn to break it across his knee. All tried and all failed. Then he undid the bundle and handed them the sticks one by one. Then they had no difficulty at all in breaking them. "There, my boys," said he, "united you will be more than a match for your enemies, but if you quarrel and separate, your weakness will put you at the mercy of those who attack you." Union is strength.

HEAVEN AND HELL

A man spoke with the Lord about heaven and hell. The Lord said to the man, "Come, I will show you hell."

They entered a room where a group of famished people sat around a huge pot of cooking stew. Everyone in the room was starving and desperate. Each person held a spoon that reached the pot. However, each spoon had a handle so much longer than their arms; it could not be used to get the stew into their own mouths. The suffering was terrible.

"Come now, I will show you heaven," the Lord said.

They entered another room identical to the first, including the big pot of stew, the group of people, and the same long-handled spoons. But here everyone was happy and well nourished.

"I don't understand," said the man. "Why is everyone happy here and miserable in the other room? Everything is the same."

"Here," said the Lord, "they have learned to feed each other."

OLD WARWICK

This story originally appeared in the play *Some Folks Feel the Rain.*[2]

A man became lost while driving through the country. As he tried to read a map, he accidentally drove off the road into a ditch. Though he wasn't injured, his car was stuck deep in the mud. Seeing a farmhouse nearby, the man walked over to ask for help. "Warwick can get you out of the ditch," the farmer said, pointing to an old mule standing in a field. The man looked at the haggard mule and then looked back at the farmer, who just stood there nodding. "Yup, old Warwick can do the job."

The man figured he had nothing to lose, so the two men and Warwick made their way back to the ditch. After the farmer hitched the old mule to the car, he snapped the reins and shouted. "Pull, Fred! Pull, Jack! Pull, Ted! Pull, Warwick!" With very little effort, the lone mule pulled the car from the ditch. The man was amazed. He thanked the farmer, patted the mule, and asked, "Why did you call out all those other names before you called Warwick?"

The farmer grinned and said, "Old Warwick is just about blind. As long as he believes he's part of a team, he doesn't mind pulling."

MODESTY

THE EMPEROR'S NEW CLOTHES
HANS CHRISTIAN ANDERSON

Once upon a time, there lived a vain emperor whose only worry in life was to dress in elegant clothes. He changed clothes almost every hour and loved to show them off to his people.

Word of the emperor's refined habits spread over his kingdom and beyond. Two scoundrels who had heard of the emperor's vanity decided to take advantage of it. They introduced themselves at the gates of the palace with a scheme in mind.

"We are two very good tailors, and after many years of research we have invented an extraordinary method to weave a cloth so light and fine that it looks invisible. As a matter of fact it is invisible to anyone who is too stupid and incompetent to appreciate its quality."

The chief of the guards heard the scoundrel's strange story and sent for the court chamberlain. The chamberlain notified the prime minister, who ran to the emperor and disclosed the incredible news. The emperor's curiosity got the better of him and he decided to see the two scoundrels.

"Besides being invisible, Your Highness, this cloth will be woven in colors and patterns created especially for you." The emperor gave the two men a bag of gold coins in exchange for their promise to begin working on the fabric immediately.

"Just tell us what you need to get started and we'll give it to you." The two scoundrels asked for a loom, silk, and gold thread, and then pretended to begin working. The emperor thought he had spent his money quite well: in addition to getting a new extraordinary suit, he would discover which of his subjects were ignorant and incompetent.

A few days later, he called the wise, old prime minister, who was considered by everyone as a man with common sense.

"Go and see how the work is proceeding," the emperor told him, "and come back to let me know."

The prime minister was welcomed by the two scoundrels.

"We're almost finished, but we need a lot more gold thread. Here, Excellency! Admire the colors, feel the softness!" The old man bent over the loom and tried to see the fabric that was not there. He felt cold sweat on his forehead.

"I can't see anything," he thought. "If I see nothing, that means I'm stupid! Or worse—incompetent!" If the prime minister admitted that he didn't see anything, he would be discharged from his office.

"What a marvelous fabric," he said then. "I'll certainly tell the emperor." The two scoundrels rubbed their hands gleefully. They had almost made it. They asked for more thread to finish the work.

Finally, the emperor received the announcement that the two tailors had come to take all the measurements needed to sew his new suit.

"Come in," the emperor ordered. Even as they bowed, the two scoundrels pretended to be holding large roll of fabric.

"Here it is Your Highness, the result of our labor," the scoundrels said. "We have worked night and day but, at last, the most beautiful fabric in the world is ready for you. Look at the colors and feel how fine it is." Of course, the emperor did not see any colors and could not feel any cloth between his fingers. He panicked and felt like fainting. Luckily, the throne was right behind him and he sat down. When he realized that no one could know that he did not see the fabric, he felt better. Nobody would find out he was stupid and incompetent. The emperor didn't know that everybody else around him thought and did the very same thing.

The farce continued as the two scoundrels had foreseen it would. Once they had taken the measurements, the two began cutting the air with scissors while sewing with their needles an invisible cloth.

"Your Highness, you'll have to take off your clothes to try on your new ones." The two scoundrels draped the new clothes on him and then held up a mirror. The emperor was embarrassed but since none of his bystanders were, he felt relieved.

"Yes, this is a beautiful suit and it looks very good on me," the emperor said, trying to look comfortable. "You've done a fine job."

"Your Majesty," the prime minister said, "we have a request for you. The people have found out about this extraordinary fabric, and they are anxious to see you in your new suit." The emperor was doubtful showing himself naked to the people, but then he abandoned his fears. After all, no one would know about it except the ignorant and the incompetent.

"All right," he said. "I will grant the people this privilege." He summoned his carriage and a ceremonial parade formed. A group of dignitaries walked at the very front of the procession and anxiously scrutinized the faces of the people in the street. All the people had gathered in the main square, pushing and shoving to get a better look. Applause welcomed the regal procession. Everyone wanted to know how stupid or incompetent his or her neighbor was but, as the emperor passed, a strange murmur rose from the crowd.

Everyone said, loud enough for the others to hear: "Look at the emperor's new clothes. They're beautiful!"

"What a marvelous train!"

"And the colors! The colors of that beautiful fabric! I have never seen anything like it in my life!" They all tried to conceal their disappointment at not being able to see the clothes, and since nobody was willing to admit his own stupidity and incompetence, they all behaved as the two scoundrels had predicted.

A child, however, who had no important job and could only see things as his eyes showed them to him, went up to the carriage.

"The emperor is naked," he said.

"Fool!" his father reprimanded, running after him. "Don't talk nonsense!" He grabbed his child and took him away. But the boy's remark, which had been heard by the bystanders, was repeated over and over again until everyone cried:

"The boy is right! The emperor is naked! It's true!"

The emperor realized that the people were right but could not admit to it. He thought it better to continue the procession under the illusion that anyone who couldn't see his clothes was either stupid or incompetent. He stood stiffly on his carriage, while behind him a page held his imaginary mantle.

TOLERANCE

DON'T BE SO QUICK TO JUDGE

There was a man who had four sons. He wanted his sons to learn not to judge things too quickly. He sent them each on a quest to go and look at a pear tree that was a great distance away.

The first son went in the winter, the second in the spring, the third in summer, and the youngest son in the fall.

When they had all gone and come back, he called them together to describe what they had seen.

The first son said that the tree was ugly, bent, and twisted.

The second son said it was covered with green buds and full of promise.

The third son disagreed; he said it was laden with blossoms that smelled sweet and looked beautiful. It was the most graceful thing he had ever seen.

The fourth son disagreed with all of them; he said it was ripe and drooping with fruit, full of life and fulfillment.

The man then explained to his sons that they were all right, because they had each seen but only one season in the tree's life.

He told them that you cannot judge a tree, or a person, by only one season, and that the essence of who they are and the pleasure, joy, and love that come from that life can only be measured at the end, when all the seasons are up.

If you give up when it's winter, you will miss the promise of your spring, the beauty of your summer, the fulfillment of your fall.

BUILDING BRIDGES

Once upon a time, two brothers who lived on adjoining farms fell into conflict. It was the first serious rift in forty years of farming side by side, sharing machinery, and trading labor and goods as needed without a hitch in their relationship.

Then the long collaboration fell apart. It began with a small misunderstanding and it grew into a major difference. Finally it exploded into an exchange of bitter words followed by weeks of silence.

One morning there was a knock on John's door. He opened it to find a man with a carpenter's toolbox. "I'm looking for a few days' work," he said. "Perhaps you would have a few small jobs here and there. Could I help you?"

"Yes," said the older brother. "I do have a job for you. Look across the creek at that farm. That's my neighbor, in fact, it's my younger brother. Last week there was a meadow between us, and he took his bulldozer to the river levee and now there is a creek between us. Well, he may have done this to spite me, but I'll go him one better. See that pile of lumber curing by the barn? I want you to build me a fence—an eight-foot fence—so I won't need to see his place anymore. Cool him down, anyhow."

The carpenter said, "I think I understand the situation. Show me the nails and the posthole digger and I'll be able to do a job that pleases you."

The older brother had to go to town for supplies, so he helped the carpenter get the materials ready and then he was off for the day.

The carpenter worked hard all that day measuring, sawing, nailing.

About sunset when the farmer returned, the carpenter had just finished his job. The farmer's eyes opened wide, and his jaw dropped.

There was no fence there at all. It was a bridge, a bridge stretching from one side of the creek to the other! A fine piece of work—handrails and all—and the neighbor, his younger brother, was coming across, his hand outstretched.

"You are quite a fellow to build this bridge after all I've said and done."

The two brothers stood at each end of the bridge, and then they met in the middle, taking each other's hand. They turned to see the carpenter hoist his toolbox on his shoulder. "No, wait! Stay a few days. I've a lot of other projects for you," said the older brother.

"I'd love to stay on," the carpenter said. "But I have many more bridges to build."

TRUTH

THE EMPEROR'S SEED

Once there was an emperor in the Far East who was growing old and knew it was coming time to choose his successor. Instead of choosing one of his assistants or one of his own children, he decided to do something different.

He called all the young people in the kingdom together one day. He said, "It has come time for me to step down and to choose the next emperor. I have decided to choose one of you." The kids were shocked! The emperor continued. "I am going to give each one of you a seed today. One seed. It is a very special seed. I want you to go home, plant the seed, water it, and come back here one year from today with what you have grown from this one seed. I will then judge the plants that you bring to me, and the one I choose will be the next emperor of the kingdom!"

There was one boy named Ling who was there that day and he, like the others, received a seed. He went home and excitedly told his mother the whole story. She helped him get a pot and some planting soil, and he planted the seed and watered it carefully. Every day he would water it and watch to see if it had grown.

After about three weeks, some of the other youths began to talk about their seeds and the plants that were beginning to grow. Ling kept going home and checking his seed, but nothing ever grew. Three weeks, four weeks, five weeks went by. Still nothing.

By now others were talking about their plants, but Ling didn't have a plant, and he felt like a failure. Six months went by—still, nothing in Ling's pot. He just knew he had killed his seed. Everyone else had trees and tall plants, but he had nothing. Ling didn't say anything to his friends. He just kept waiting for his seed to grow.

A year finally went by, and all the youths of the kingdom brought their plants to the emperor for inspection. Ling told his mother that he wasn't going to take an empty pot. She encouraged him to go and to take his pot, and to be honest about what happened. Ling felt sick to his stomach, but he knew his mother was right. He took his empty pot to the palace.

When Ling arrived, he was amazed at the variety of plants grown by all the other youths. They were beautiful, in all shapes and sizes. Ling put his empty pot on the floor and many of the other kids laughed at him. A few felt sorry for him and just said, "Hey, nice try."

When the emperor arrived, he surveyed the room and greeted the young people. Ling tried to hide in the back. "My, what great plants, trees, and flowers you have grown," said the emperor. "Today, one of you will be appointed the next emperor!"

All of a sudden, the emperor spotted Ling at the back of the room with his empty pot. He ordered his guards to bring him to the front. Ling was terrified. "The emperor knows I'm a failure! Maybe he will have me killed!"

When Ling got to the front, the emperor asked his name. "My name is Ling," he replied. All the kids were laughing and making fun of him. The emperor asked everyone to quiet down. He looked at Ling, and then announced to the crowd, "Behold your new emperor! His name is Ling!" Ling couldn't believe it. Ling couldn't even grow his seed. How could he be the new emperor?

Then the emperor said, "One year ago today, I gave everyone here a seed. I told you to take the seed, plant it, water it, and bring it back to me today. However, I gave all of you all boiled seeds that would not grow. All of you, except Ling, have brought me trees and plants and flowers. When you found that the seed would not grow, you substituted another seed for the one I gave you. Ling was the only one with the courage and honesty to bring me a pot with my seed in it. Therefore, he is the one who will be the new emperor!

UNDER THE LION'S SKIN
AESOP

A donkey found a lion's skin and put it on. In this frightening disguise, he grazed in a farmer's field. He amused himself by frightening all the animals he met. He felt so powerful!

Along came a fox. The donkey under the lion's skin tried to frighten him. The donkey stood tall under the skin and let out a sound that he thought would resemble a roar. Alas, his donkey voice was all that was heard.

The fox laughed and said, "Silly donkey, if you really want to frighten me, you'll have to disguise your bray. Clothes *may* disguise a fool, you know, but his words always give him away!"

THE MONKEY AND THE DOLPHIN
AESOP

One day long ago, some sailors set out to sea in their sailing ship. One of them brought his pet monkey along for the long journey.

When they were far out at sea, a terrible storm overturned their ship. Everyone fell into the sea, and the monkey was sure that he would drown. Suddenly a dolphin appeared and picked him up.

They soon reached the island and the monkey came down from the dolphin's back. The dolphin asked the monkey, "Do you know this place?"

The monkey replied, "Yes, I do. In fact, the king of the island is my best friend. Do you know that I am actually a prince?"

Knowing that no one lived on the island, the dolphin said, "Well, well, so you are a prince! Now you can be a king!" The monkey asked, "How can I be a king?"

As the dolphin started swimming away, he answered, "That is easy. As you are the only creature on this island, you will naturally be the king!"

The moral of the story is those who lie and boast may end up in trouble. It's always best to tell the truth.

INITIATIVE

FIELD OF DREAMS

In the movie *Field of Dreams*, the elderly doctor named Moonlight Graham was asked what it was like to have his entire major league career consist of playing just one inning for the New York Giants and never getting an opportunity to bat. His response should make all of us think of the opportunities we are given. "It was like coming this close to your dreams," he said, holding his fingers slightly apart, "and then watching them brush past you like a stranger in a crowd. At the time, you don't think much of it. You know… we just don't recognize significant moments of our lives while they are happening. Back then, I thought there would be other days. I didn't realize that was the only day."

Being an athlete and a teammate only lasts so long, and it can end on any day. Enjoy every day of the experience. This can be one of those moments or seasons you look back on as the great memory of your life. How sad it would be to look back on it and realize that you have missed the journey.

THE 100TH MONKEY
KEN KEYES JR.

The Japanese monkey *Macaca Fuscata* had been observed in the wild on Japanese Islands for a period of over thirty years.

In 1952, on the island of Koshima, Japan, scientists were providing over five hundred monkeys with sweet potatoes dropped in the sand. The monkeys liked the taste of the raw sweet potatoes, but they found the sand unpleasant. An eighteen-month-old female named Imo found she could solve the problem by washing the potatoes in a nearby stream. She taught this trick to her mother. Her playmates also learned this new way and they taught their mothers, too.

This cultural innovation was gradually picked up by various monkeys before the eyes of the scientists. Between 1952 and 1958, most of the young monkeys had learned to wash the sandy sweet potatoes to make them more palatable. Only the adults who imitated their children learned this social improvement. By the autumn of 1958, sixty-two young monkeys and thirty-seven adult monkeys, a total of ninety-nine monkeys, were using the newly learned behavior. By far the vast majority of older adult monkeys kept eating the sweet potatoes with sand on them.

Then something startling took place on October 28, 1958. For nearly six years, ninety-nine of the more than five hundred monkeys had been washing the sand off their sweet potatoes and enjoying a dirt-free meal, while the others suffered through crunching sand in their teeth. Then it happened! That morning, the hundredth monkey learned to wash potatoes.

By that evening, almost every monkey on the island was washing sweet potatoes before eating them. The added energy of this hundredth monkey somehow created an ideological breakthrough! Call it critical mass; call it the tipping point; the cultural change spread through the whole population. But that wasn't all.

The most surprising thing observed by these scientists was that the habit of washing sweet potatoes then jumped over the sea. Colonies of monkeys on other islands and the mainland troop of monkeys at Takasakiyama began washing their sweet potatoes.

The scientists theorized that when a certain critical number in a population achieves awareness, this new awareness might be communicated from mind to mind.

This is called the "Hundredth Monkey Phenomenon."[1]

The Hundredth Monkey Phenomenon means that when only a limited number of people know of a new way and better way to live, the new way might remained confined to the limited group for some time. There is a point at which if just one more person tunes in to a new awareness, the field is strengthened so that almost everyone picks up this awareness!

What do you think kept that hundredth monkey from washing his sweet potato? Stubbornness, pride, fear of change, selfishness, he didn't think washing his sweet potato was cool?

What is keeping you from joining in on making cultural changes for the good on your team, in your classroom, school, work, church, organization, or home?

Are you the hundredth monkey?

THE EAGLE AND THE CHICKEN

There's an old fable that talks about a man who found an eagle's egg and put it in a nest of a barnyard hen. The eagle hatched with the brood of chicks and grew up with them. All his life, the eagle did what the barnyard chicks did, thinking he was a barnyard chicken. He scratched the earth for worms and insects. He clucked and cackled. He would thrash his wings and fly a few feet in the air. Years passed and the eagle grew very old. One day he saw a magnificent bird above him in the cloudless sky. It glided in graceful majesty among powerful wind currents, with scarcely a beat of its strong golden wings. The old eagle looked up in awe. "Who's that?" he asked.

"That's the eagle, the king of the birds," said his neighbor. "He belongs to the sky. We belong to the earth. We're chickens."

So the eagle lived and died as a chicken, for that's what he thought he was. Most people follow chickens, act like chickens, and live out their life like chickens. You can never attain the heights of success by having unsuccessful role models. You are not going to get to greatness by listening to and emulating those who want to keep you down at their level and hold you back from achieving the highest level of competence.

THE JOBLESS TRENCH DIGGER

An elderly couple retired to the countryside, to a small, isolated cottage overlooking some rugged and rocky heathland.

One early morning, the woman saw from her window a young man dressed in working clothes walking on the road, about a hundred yards away. He was carrying a spade and a small case. He disappeared from view behind a group of trees.

The woman thought no more about it, but around the same time the following day she saw the man again, carrying his spade and a small case. Again he disappeared behind the trees.

The woman mentioned this to her husband, who said the man was probably a farmer or gamekeeper setting traps or performing some other country practice that would be perfectly normal, and not to worry.

But after several more sightings of the young man with the spade, the woman persuaded her husband to take a stroll early in the day before the man's expected arrival.

They went to the patch of trees to investigate what he was doing. There they found a surprisingly long and deep trench, rough and uneven at one end, becoming much neater and tidier towards the other end.

"How strange," the old lady said. "Why dig a trench here in such difficult rocky ground?" Her husband agreed.

Just then the young man appeared. It was earlier than his usual time.

"You're early," said the old woman, making light of their obvious curiosity. "We wondered what you are doing, and we also wondered what is in the case."

"I'm digging a trench," said the man. He continued, realizing a bigger explanation was appropriate. "I'm actually learning how to dig a good trench because the job I'm being interviewed for later today says that experience is essential. I'm getting experience. And the case…it's got my lunch in it."

He got the job.

KINDNESS

THE LION AND THE MOUSE
AESOP

Here is one of the oldest and best-loved stories of kindness paid and repaid. From it, we learn that compassion lies within the power of both the mighty and the meek. Kindness is not a feeble virtue.

One day a great lion lay asleep in the sunshine. A little mouse ran across its paw and wakened the lion. The great lion was going to eat him up when the little mouse cried, "Oh, please, let me go, sir. Someday I may help you."

The lion laughed at the thought that the little mouse could be of any use to him. However, he was a good-natured lion and he set the mouse free. Not long after, the lion was caught in a net. He tugged and pulled with all his might, but the ropes were too strong. Then he roared loudly. The little mouse heard him, and ran to the spot. "Be still, dear Lion, and I will set you free. I will gnaw the ropes."

With his sharp little teeth, the mouse cut the ropes, and the lion came out of the net. "You laughed at me once," said the mouse. "You thought I was too little to do you a good turn, but see, you owe your life to a poor little mouse."

A SIMPLE ACT OF KINDNESS
JOHN W. SCHLATTER

Mark was walking home from school one day when he noticed the boy ahead of him had tripped and dropped all of the books he was carrying, along with two sweaters, a baseball bat, a glove, and a small tape recorder. Mark knelt down and helped the boy pick up the scattered articles. Since they were going the same way, he helped carry part of the burden. As they walked, Mark discovered the boy's name was Bill, that he loved video games, baseball, and history, and that he was having lots of trouble with his other subjects and that he had just broken up with his girlfriend. They arrived at Bill's home first and Bill invited Mark in to have a Coke and to watch some television. The afternoon passed pleasantly with a few laughs and some shared small talk; then Mark went home. They continued to see each other around school, had lunch together once or twice, and then both graduated from junior high school. They ended up in the same high school where they had brief contacts over the years. Finally, the long-awaited senior year came and three weeks before graduation, Bill asked Mark if they could talk.

Bill reminded him of the day years ago when they had first met. "Did you ever wonder why I was carrying so many things home that day?" asked Bill. "You see, I cleaned out my locker because I didn't want to leave a mess for anyone else. I had stored away some of my mother's sleeping pills and I was going home to commit suicide. After we spent some time together talking and laughing, I realized that if I had killed myself, I would have missed that time and so many others that might follow. So you see, Mark, when you picked up those books that day, you did a lot more than just pick up books. You saved my life."[1]

THE MASK

Don't be fooled by the face I wear, for I wear a thousand masks, and none of them are me. Don't be fooled, for goodness' sake, don't be fooled. I give you the impression that I'm secure, that confidence is my name and coolness is my game, and that I need no one. But don't believe me.

Beneath dwells the real me in confusion, in aloneness, in fear. That's why I create a mask to hide behind, to shield me from the glance that knows, but such a glance is precisely my salvation. That is, if it's followed by acceptance, if it's followed by love. It's the only thing that can liberate me from my own self-built prison walls. I'm afraid that deep down I'm nothing and that I'm just no good, and that you will reject me.

And so begins the parade of masks. I idly chatter to you. I tell you everything that's really nothing and nothing of what's everything, of what's crying within me.

Please listen carefully and try to hear what I'm not saying. I'd really like to be genuine and spontaneous, and me. But you've got to help me. You've got to hold out your hand.

Each time you're kind, gentle, and encouraging, each time you try to understand because you really care, my heart begins to grow wings— feeble wings—but wings.

With your sensitivity and sympathy and your power of understanding, you alone can release me from my shallow world of uncertainty.

It will not be easy for you. The nearer you approach me, the more blindly I may strike back.

I'm told that love is stronger than strong walls, and in this lays my only hope.

Please try to beat down these walls with firm but gentle hands for a child is very sensitive.

Who am I? You wonder. I am every man or woman you meet, and I am also you.

KNOWLEDGE

THE CHESS PLAYERS

Two men had played chess regularly together for several years. They were quite evenly matched and there was keen rivalry between them. Then one man began to beat his rival nearly every time they played. The other man was completely at a loss to understand this phenomenon. He was expecting his game to improve because he was reading a four-volume set on how to play chess! After much thought, he came up with an idea. He sent the books to his friend as a gift—and it was not long before they were evenly matched again! Knowledge comes through experience. Mere information is not knowledge. On the contrary, it cannot give the clarity that knowledge gives to the mind, and it may even confuse more because a confused mind is burdened with it.

THE HIDDEN KNOWLEDGE

This is a beautiful story a Sioux friend told me. The Creator gathered all of creation and said, "I want to hide something from the humans until they are ready for it. It is the realization that they create their own reality."

The eagle said, "Give it to me, I will take it to the moon."

The Creator said, "No. One day they will go there and find it."

The salmon said, "I will hide it on the bottom of the ocean."

"No. They will go there too."

The buffalo said, "I will bury it on the great plains."

The Creator said, "They will cut into the skin of the earth and find it even there."

Then Grandmother Mole, who lives in the breast of Mother Earth, and who has no physical eyes but sees with spiritual eyes, said, "Put it inside them."

And the Creator said, "It is done."

THE SHEPHERD STORY

A shepherd was tending his flock in a field, when a new sports car screeched to a stop in a cloud of dust on the road nearby. The driver, a young man in expensive designer clothes and sunglasses, leaned out of the window and shouted to the shepherd, "If I tell you exactly how many sheep you have here, can I take one?"

The shepherd looked up slowly up at the young man, then looked at his peaceful flock, and calmly answered, "Sure, why not?"

The young man stepped out of his car holding a state-of-the-art iPhone, with which he proceeded to connect to a series of websites, first calling up a satellite navigation system to pinpoint his location, then keying in the location to generate an ultra-high resolution picture of the field. After emailing the photo to an image processing facility, the processed data returned. This he fed into an online database, and enters the parameters for a report. Within another few seconds, a miniature printer in the car produced a full color report containing several pages of analysis and results. The young man studied the data for a few more seconds and then he returned to the shepherd.

"You have exactly one-thousand, five-hundred, and eighty-six sheep, including three rams, and seven-hundred and twenty-two lambs."

"That's right," says the shepherd, mildly impressed. "Well, I guess that means you get to take one of my sheep."

The young man makes his choice and loads the animal onto the back seat of his car, at which the shepherd says, almost as an afterthought, "Hey there, if I can tell you what your business is, will you give me back my sheep?"

The young man, feeling confident, agrees.

"You're a consultant," says the shepherd.

"Wow, that's right," says the young man, taken aback, "How did you guess that?"

"No guessing required," answers the shepherd, "You showed up here even though nobody called you. You took a fee for giving me an answer that I already know to a question I never asked, and you know nothing about my business.

"Now give me back my dog."

LEADERSHIP

THE GOLDEN BUDDHA
JACK CANFIELD

In Bangkok, Thailand, there are many temples of Buddha, but there is one temple that stands out above all the others. It is not the size (it is about the size of a two-car garage) of the temple that is so impressive. Rather the temple of the Golden Buddha is famous for what is inside: a solid gold statue of the Buddha that stands almost eleven feet high and weighs over two-and-a-half tons. The history of the statue is fascinating, and has a lesson for teams.

In 1957 a certain monastery had to be relocated to make way for a highway. One of the many art objects in the monastery that had to be moved was the massive clay statue of the Buddha. When a crane lifted the clay statue, it developed serious cracks. It turns out that underneath the clay was the Golden Buddha. Historians believe that to keep an invading army from carrying it away as stolen treasure, it had been concealed for several hundred years prior to its discovery.

The point is this: Teams are like that statue. There is gold inside every team member, even though that gold may be disguised by a layer of human clay. Our job as leaders, when trying to create great teams, is to penetrate that layer of clay, uncover the gold, and reveal the value and worth that is at the core of every person making up the team. When team leaders can see the worth of each person and provide an enlarged vision for the value that person can bring to the team, the team will accomplish more than it ever thought possible.[1]

WE CAN LEARN A LOT FROM GEESE
ANGELES ARRIEN

Lesson 1: Fly Together

It's truly a marvelous sight to see a group of geese flying together in perfect V formation. Research has shown that as each goose flaps its wings it creates an intense uplift for the birds behind it. Further studies state that this "teamwork" adds seventy-one percent more flying range compared to a goose flying on its own.

Moral of the Story: Partnerships and teamwork rule the day. The days of the Lone Ranger are long gone (bad example, as even the Lone Ranger had Tonto, but you know what I mean). If you surround yourself with excellent people, you're far more likely to succeed than if you attempt to go at it alone.

Lesson 2: Stay in Formation

If you've watched geese fly, you've likely seen one fall out of formation. When this happens, the fallen away goose begins to struggle mightily until it manages to fight its way back into formation.

Moral of the Story: Once you've established a good team, stay together and work together. Sure, times will get tough and you may become annoyed with one another from time to time, but synergy cannot be created by a single person working in isolation.

Lesson 3: Rotate

While flying in V formation the lead goose eventually tires and rotates to the back of the pack to recharge its battery while another goose goes to the front.

Moral of the Story: It's important to share the load amongst team members. It's also important to ensure that all workers are cross-trained and able to perform multiple tasks.

Lesson 4: Honk

While it's not always possible to hear from the ground, geese are a noisy bunch when flying in V formation. There are several theories of why this is. One theory is the geese honk to encourage each other. An other theory hypothesizes the honking is used to communicate where each goose is. You know, hurry up pal (honk, honk). I'm right on your feathers.

Moral of the Story: No matter the reason why geese honk, it goes without saying that we should always communicate with one another, offering encouragement as needed. We should also have ways to communicate when something is not right. This can be likened to the way lean companies "pull the rip cord" when a problem arises.

Lesson 5: Leave No Goose Behind

Whenever a goose becomes unable to fly (becomes sick, gets a bullet in the belly, etc.) two other geese fall out of formation and stay with their fallen comrade until the impaired goose is able to fly or dies.

Moral of the Story: The best teams I've ever been part of were made of people who genuinely cared for each other and would always help each other no matter the situation. It seems geese figured this out a long time ago.[2]

THE SOLDIERS AND THE TRENCH

The story goes that sometime over 200 years ago, a man in civilian clothes rode close to a battlefield and past a small group of exhausted battle-weary soldiers digging an obviously important defensive position. The section leader, making no effort to help, was shouting orders, threatening punishment if the work was not completed within the hour.

"Why are you are not helping?" asked the stranger on horseback.

"I am in charge. The men do as I tell them," said the section leader, adding, "Help them yourself if you feel strongly about it."

To the section leader's surprise the stranger dismounted and helped the men until the job was finished.

Before leaving, the stranger congratulated the men for their work, and approached the puzzled section leader.

"You should notify top command next time your rank prevents you from supporting your men, and I will provide a more permanent solution," said the stranger.

Up close, the section leader now recognized General Washington . . . and also the lesson he'd just been taught.

LOYALTY

AN OLD MAN AND HIS DOG
ROD SERLING

An old man and his dog were walking along a country road, enjoying the scenery, when it suddenly occurred to the man that he had died. He remembered dying. He also realized that the dog had been dead for many years. He wondered where the road would lead them. They continued onward.

After a while, they came to a high, white stone wall along one side of the road. It looked like fine marble. At the top of a long hill, the wall was broken by a tall, white arch that gleamed in the sunlight. When he was standing before it, he saw a magnificent gate in the arch that looked like mother of pearl, and the street that led to the gate looked like pure gold. He was pleased that he had finally arrived at heaven. The man and his dog walked toward the gate. As he got closer, he saw someone sitting at a beautifully carved desk off to one side. When he was close enough, he called out, "Excuse me, but is this heaven?"

"Yes, it is, sir," the man answered.

"Wow! Would you happen to have some water?" the man asked.

"Of course, sir. Come on in and I'll have some ice water brought right up." The gatekeeper gestured to his rear, and the huge gate began to open.

"I assume my friend can come in," the man said, gesturing toward his dog. But the reply was, "I'm sorry, sir, but we don't accept pets." The man thought about it, then thanked the gatekeeper, turned back toward the road, and continued in the direction he had been going.

After another long walk, he reached the top of another long hill, and he came to a dirt road that led through a farm gate. There was no fence, and it looked as if the gate had never been closed. Grass had grown up around it. As he approached the gate, he saw a man just inside, sitting in the shade of a tree in a rickety old chair, reading a book. "Excuse me!" he called to the reader. "Do you have any water?"

"Yeah, sure, there's a pump over there," the man said, pointing to a place that he couldn't see from outside the gate. "Come on in and make yourself at home."

"How about my friend here?" the traveler gestured to the dog.

"He's welcome too, and there's a bowl by the pump," he said. They walked through the gate and, sure enough, there was an old-fashioned hand pump with a dipper hanging on it and a bowl next to it on the ground. The man filled the bowl for his dog, and then took a long drink himself.

When both were satisfied, he and the dog walked back toward the man, who was sitting under the tree waiting for them, and asked, "What do you call this place?" the traveler asked.

"This is heaven," was the answer.

"Well, that's confusing," the traveler said. "It certainly doesn't look like heaven, and there's another man down the road who said that place was heaven."

"Oh, you mean the place with the gold street and pearly gates?

"Yes, it was beautiful."

"Nope. That's hell."

"Doesn't it offend you for them to use the name of heaven like that?"

"No. I can see how you might think so, but it actually saves us a lot of time. They screen out the people who are willing to leave their best friends behind."[1]

RESPECT

AN IMPORTANT LIFE LESSON

During my second month of nursing school, our professor gave us a pop quiz. I was a conscientious student and had breezed through the questions, until I read the last one: "What is the first name of the woman who cleans the school?" Surely, this was some kind of joke.

I had seen the cleaning woman several times. She was tall, dark-haired, and in her fifties, but how would I know her name? I handed in my paper, leaving the last question blank.

Just before class ended, one student asked if the last question would count toward our quiz grade. "Absolutely," said the professor. "In your careers, you will meet many people. All are significant. They deserve your attention and care, even if all you do is smile and say 'hello.' "

I've never forgotten that lesson. I also learned her name was Dorothy. [1]

RESPONSIBILITY

I DON'T WANT TO GO TO SCHOOL

A mother repeatedly called upstairs for her son to get up, get dressed and get ready for school. It was a familiar routine, especially at exam time.

"I feel sick," said the voice from the bedroom.

"You are not sick. Get up and get ready," called the mother, walking up the stairs and hovering outside the bedroom door.

"I hate school and I'm not going," said the voice from the bedroom, "I'm always getting things wrong, making mistakes, and getting told off. Nobody likes me. I've got no friends. We have too many tests and they are too confusing. It's all just pointless, and I'm not going to school ever again."

"I'm sorry, but you are going to school," said the mother through the door, continuing encouragingly, "Really, mistakes are how we learn and develop. Please try not to take criticism so personally. I can't believe that nobody likes you. You have lots of friends at school. And yes, all those tests can be confusing, but we are all tested in many ways throughout our lives, so all of this experience at school is useful for life in general. Besides, you have to go; you are the head teacher."

THE FROG AND THE SCORPION
AESOP

Once upon a time, a scorpion wanted to cross a brook. On the bank, he saw a frog and asked if the frog would give him a ride to the other side.

"Oh no," says the frog, "If I carry you on my back you will sting me."

"But why would I sting you when we would both surely perish," replied the scorpion.

The frog eventually conceded that the scorpion had a point, and agreed to the request.

Halfway across, the scorpion stung the frog, and they both began to drown.

"But why did you break your word and sting me, knowing it would be certain death for us both?" cried the frog.

"Because it is in my nature," said the scorpion.

SELF-RESPECT

IDENTITY
JULIO NOBOA JR.

Let them be as flowers: always watered, fed, guarded, and admired, but harnessed to a pot of dirt. I'd rather be a tall, ugly weed, clinging on cliffs, like an eagle that is wind-wavering above high, jagged rocks. To have broken through the surface of stone, to live, to feel exposed to the madness of the vast, eternal sky. To be swayed by the breezes of an ancient sea, carrying my soul, my seed, beyond the mountains of time or into the abyss of the bizarre. I'd rather be unseen, and if then shunned by everyone, than to be a pleasant-smelling flower, growing in clusters in the fertile valley, where they're praised, handled, and plucked by greedy, human hands. I'd rather smell of musty, green stench than of sweet, fragrant lilac. If I could stand alone, strong and free, I'd rather be a tall, ugly weed.

HOW MUCH IS A HOMELESS MAN WORTH?

"The homeless man lying in the gutter is just as valuable as the most admired movie star." —Kent Crockett

A well-known speaker began his seminar by holding up a twenty-dollar bill. He asked everyone at the conference, "Who would like this new twenty-dollar bill?" Hands went up all over the room.

He said, "I'm going to give this to one of you, but first I need to crumple it." He wadded up the bill and asked, "Who still wants it?"

Hands went up all around the room. The speaker dropped the bill and ground it into the floor with his shoe. He picked up the crumpled, dirty bill. "Now who wants it?" Everyone still lifted a hand.

"Friends, you have all learned a valuable lesson," the speaker concluded. "No matter what I did to the money, you still want it because its value hasn't changed. Even though the bill is crumpled and dirty, it's still worth twenty dollars."

Although someone may have been misused and abused, he or she still has infinite worth. Every person is precious in God's sight.

Do you see others—and yourself—as priceless?

ROCKEFELLER'S LOAN

The business executive was deep in debt and could see no way out.

Creditors were closing in on him. Suppliers were demanding payment. He sat on the park bench, head in hands, wondering if anything could save his company from bankruptcy.

Suddenly an old man appeared before him.

"I can see that something is troubling you," he said.

After listening to the executive's woes, the old man said, "I believe I can help you."

He asked the man his name, wrote out a check, and pushed it into his hand saying, "Take this money. Meet me here exactly one year from today, and you can pay me back at that time."

Then he turned and disappeared as quickly as he had come.

The business executive saw in his hand a check for $500,000, signed by John D. Rockefeller, who was at that time one of the richest men in the world!

"I can erase my money worries in an instant!" the executive realized. Instead, the executive decided to put the un-cashed check in his safe. He thought that just knowing it was there might give him the strength to work out a way to save his business.

With renewed optimism, he negotiated better deals and extended terms of payment. He closed several big sales. Within a few months, he was out of debt and making money once again.

Exactly one year later, he returned to the park with the uncashed check. At the agreed-upon time, the old man appeared. Just as the executive was about to hand back the check and share his success story, a nurse came running up and grabbed the old man.

"I'm so glad I caught him!" she cried. "I hope he hasn't been bothering you. He's always escaping from the rest home and telling people he's John D. Rockefeller."

She led the old man away by the arm.

The astonished executive just stood there, stunned. All year long he'd been wheeling and dealing, buying and selling, convinced he had half a million dollars behind him.

Suddenly, he realized that it wasn't the money, real or imagined, that had turned his life around. It was his newfound self-respect that gave him the power to achieve anything he went after.

PATRIOTISM

SACK LUNCHES
BEVERLY BASS, AS TOLD BY DENNY KUKICH

I put my carry-on in the luggage compartment and sat down in my assigned seat. It was going to be a long flight. *I'm glad I have a good book to read. Perhaps I will get a short nap,* I thought.

Just before take-off, a line of soldiers came down the aisle and filled all the vacant seats. I was totally surrounded. I decided to start a conversation.

"Where are you headed?" I asked the soldier seated nearest to me.

"Petawawa. We'll be there for two weeks for special training, and then we're being deployed to Afghanistan."

After flying for about an hour, an announcement was made that sack lunches were available for five dollars. It would be several hours before we reached the east, and I quickly decided a lunch would help pass the time.

As I reached for my wallet, I overheard a soldier ask his buddy if he planned to buy lunch. "No, that seems like a lot of money for a sack lunch. Probably wouldn't be worth five bucks. I'll wait till we get to base." His friend agreed.

I looked around at the other soldiers. None were buying lunch. I walked to the back of the plane and handed the flight attendant a fifty-dollar bill. "Take a lunch to all those soldiers."

She grabbed my arms and squeezed tightly. Her eyes were wet with tears. She thanked me. "My son was a soldier in Iraq; it's almost like you are doing it for him."

Picking up ten lunch sacks, she headed up the aisle to where the soldiers were seated. She stopped at my seat and asked, "Which do you like best—beef or chicken?"

Chicken," I replied, wondering why she asked. She turned and went to the front of plane, returning a minute later with a dinner plate from first class.

"This is your thanks."

After we finished eating, I went again to the back of the plane, heading for the rest room. A man stopped me. "I saw what you did. I want to be part of it. Here, take this." He handed me twenty-five dollars.

Soon after I returned to my seat, I saw the flight captain coming down the aisle, looking at the aisle numbers as he walked. I hoped he was not looking for me, but noticed he was looking at the numbers only on my side of the plane. When he got to my row, he stopped, smiled, held out his hand, and said, "I want to shake your hand." Quickly, unfastening my seatbelt, I stood and took the Captain's hand. With a booming voice he said, "I was a soldier and I was a military pilot. Once, someone bought me a lunch. It was an act of kindness I never forgot." I was embarrassed when all the passengers applauded.

Later I walked to the front of the plane so I could stretch my legs. A man seated about six rows in front of me reached out his hand, wanting to shake mine. He left another twenty-five dollars in my palm.

When we landed, I gathered my belongings and started to deplane. Waiting just inside the airplane door was a man who stopped me, put something in my shirt pocket, turned, and walked away without saying a word. Another twenty-five dollars!

Upon entering the terminal, I saw the soldiers gathering for their trip to the base. I walked over to them and handed them seventy-five dollars. "It will take you some time to reach the base. It will be about time for a sandwich. God bless you."

Ten young men left that flight feeling the love and respect of their fellow travelers.

As I walked briskly to my car, I whispered a prayer for their safe return. The soldiers were giving their all for our country. I could only give them a couple of meals. It seemed so little.

A veteran is someone who, at one point in his life, wrote a blank check made payable to "The United States of America" for an amount of "up to and including my life."

That is honor. And there are too many people in this country who no longer understand it.

THE TOMB OF THE UNKNOWN SOLDIER

The Tomb of the Unknown Soldier represents all the American service men and women who have died. Guarding that tomb is an honor bestowed on a few committed men.

Who are these men? The physical traits are specific:

- They must be between five-foot, ten inches and six-foot, two inches tall.
- Their waist size cannot exceed thirty inches. As they stand duty, their rifle is always carried on the shoulder away from the tomb and the gloves are always moistened to prevent losing their grip on the rifle. The guards are changed every thirty minutes, twenty-four hours a day, 365 days a year. Each guard takes exactly twenty-one steps on their walk across the front of the tomb. At the end of the pass in front of the tomb, they do an about face and pause for exactly twenty-one seconds before the return walk. The twenty-one steps and twenty-one seconds alludes to the twenty-one gun salute, which is the highest honor given to any military dignitary.
- Once they are selected to serve the Unknown Soldier:
  1. They must commit two years of their life living in barracks under the tomb.
  2. During the first six months of duty, a guard cannot talk to anyone, nor watch television.
  3. All off duty time is spent studying the 175 notable people laid to rest in Arlington National Cemetery. A guard must memorize who they are and where they are interred.
  4. Every guard spends five hours a day getting his uniforms ready for guard duty.
  5. They pledge not to drink any alcohol on or off duty, not just during that period of time, but for the remainder of their lives.
  6. They cannot swear in public for the rest of their lives.
  7. They agree never to disgrace the uniform or the tomb in any way with their behavior.

After two years, the guard receives a wreath pin, which he wears on his lapel to signify that he served as a guard of the tomb. There are only 400 currently worn. If the guard ever violates any of the commitments made, he must surrender the wreath pin.

SUFFERING A CAUSE

TEACHING ELEPHANTS TO DANCE

In his book *Teaching the Elephant to Dance*, James Belasco describes how trainers shackle young elephants with heavy chains to deeply embedded stakes. In that way the elephant learns to stay in its place. Older, powerful elephants never try to leave, even though they have the strength to pull the stake and walk away. Their conditioning has limited their movements. With only a metal bracelet around their foot attached to a short piece of chain, they stand in place; the stakes are actually gone!

Like powerful elephants, people are bound by earlier conditioned restraints. If you are suffering from the world's futility, it is a learned behavior that has taken place over time, and it is now holding back your positive influence on humanity just like the unattached chain around an elephant's foot. When the circus tent catches on fire and the elephant sees the flames and smells the smoke, it forgets its old conditioning and runs for its life. If you are suffering from futility, you need to realize that your spiritual house is on fire and you better do something about it before it burns down. It's time to remind yourself day after day, moment by moment, that you are not here on this earth just for yourself, but you have been called to a higher purpose in your service to humanity.[1]

MARTYRS OF THE MODERN ERA

Ten twentieth-century Christian martyrs are commemorated with statues at Westminster Abbey in London. The statues were unveiled before the Queen and the Duke of Edinburgh at Westminster Abbey. Church officials of different religious denominations from all over the world joined them. The martyrs chosen by the Abbey represent religious persecution and oppression in each continent. Among them are victims of the Nazism, Communism, and religious prejudice around the world.

"There has never been a time in Christian history when someone, somewhere, has not died rather than compromise with the powers of oppression, tyranny, and unbelief," Rev. Dr. Anthony Harvey, sub-dean of Westminster, told the congregation.[2]

The earliest definition of a martyr meant someone who had witnessed Jesus' life. Over time, the term martyr has come to mean someone who has suffered death at the hands of a persecutor for their faith and beliefs.

20th Century Martyrs:

- In 1918 the Grand Duchess Elizabeth of Russia was killed by the Bolsheviks.
- Manche Masemola was an Anglican catechumen from South Africa who was killed in 1928 by her parents at the age of sixteen.
- Maximilian Kolbe was canonized by the Roman Catholic Church after being killed by the Nazis in 1941.
- In 1941 Lucian Tapiede, an Anglican from Papua New Guinea, was killed during the Japanese invasion.
- Dietrich Bonhoeffer was a Lutheran pastor and theologian killed by the Nazis in 1945.
- Esther John, a Presbyterian evangelist from Pakistan, was allegedly killed by a Muslim fanatic in 1960.
- One of the world's most famous civil rights activists, Martin Luther King, a Baptist, was assassinated in 1969.
- In 1972 Wang Zhiming was killed during the Chinese Cultural Revolution. He was a pastor and evangelist.
- In 1977, Janani Luwum was assassinated during the rule of Idi Amin, in Uganda, for being an Anglican archbishop.
- Oscar Romero, a Roman Catholic Archbishop in El Salvador, was assassinated in 1980.

All of the modern martyrs spent their lives striving for a better world. But for some, achieving this rested on total non-violence regardless of the might of their opposition.

FAITHFULNESS

THE TRUE STORY OF THE FAITHFUL DOG HACHIKO
TRIWIK KURNIASARI

Akitas are considered to be among the most loyal of all dogs, and no one who has heard the amazing true story of Hachiko will disagree. In January 1924, a professor at the Japanese Imperial University brought home a two-month-old Akita puppy. Dr. Ueno named the pup Hachiko. The following year was a wonderful time for Hachiko and his new master. Akitas are large dogs, and Hachiko grew to be over ninety pounds. This beautiful white dog accompanied Dr. Ueno to the Shibuya train station every morning where Dr. Ueno would say goodbye to Hachiko and head to the university. Every day when Dr. Ueno returned home Hachiko would be waiting for him at the train station and the two would go home together. Anyone could see the powerful bond between the large Akita and his master.

If things had continued like this, the story would still be one of admirable faithfulness from a dog to its master. But that was not the fate of Dr. Ueno and his loyal Akita, Hachiko.

May 21, 1925, was like any other day for the pair. In the morning, Professor Ueno left Hachiko at Shibuya Station. When Hachiko returned to Shibuya Station in the evening, his master was nowhere to be found. Though Hachiko waited, Dr. Ueno never showed up. Dr. Ueno had died from a stroke earlier that day.

Akitas are loyal dogs, and they do not bond easily with new people. Hachiko was sent away to another area of Japan where relatives of Dr. Ueno's could take care of him. Because Hachiko had belonged to Dr. Ueno for only a little over a year, they probably hoped the Akita would make a new family with them. Hachiko didn't care. He ran away from the family and returned to the train station to wait for his master. The family realized they couldn't keep the big Akita dog from heading to Shibuya Station every day, so they gave Hachiko to Dr. Ueno's old gardener who still lived in the area.

Every evening, Hachiko would return to Shibuya Station and wait for Dr. Ueno to get off the six-o'clock train; and every day, Hachiko was disappointed. Still, he never missed a day of hoping that his master would return to him.

The commuters noticed the Akita waiting every day at the station. Some of them had known the pair when Dr. Ueno was still alive, and everyone who heard of Hachiko's story was touched. People petted him and gave him food. Months passed, then years. Still Hachiko kept his vigil. A newspaper heard about the dog and Hachiko became a Japanese celebrity. To commemorate his loyalty, a statue of the Akita was erected at Shibuya station. Hachiko was even present at the ceremony!

Despite the people's loving intentions, Hachiko basically lived as a stray. He would call no place home except where Dr. Ueno was, and since Dr. Ueno was nowhere, Hachiko had no home. He lived on the street, fought other dogs, and ate scraps and handouts. Hachiko got sick with worms and mange, but because so many people admired him, he was given treatment by a veterinarian. Hachiko became an old, scarred dog, with one ear up and one ear down, and no longer looked like the purebred Akita that he was.

It was March 1935 when Hachiko finally died. The old Akita was found in a Shibuya street. He had waited for his master for almost ten years. Many people were saddened by Hachiko's death, but others say that he was finally at peace and could go with his master wherever it is we go when we die. Hachiko's story of loyalty touched the hearts of many people all over the world. In Japan, his statue at Shibuya Station is still a popular meeting place. There is even a ceremony to remember Hachiko every year on April 8.[1]

THE GLASSES

Mother's father worked as a carpenter. On this particular day, he was building some crates for the clothes his church was sending to an orphanage in China. On his way home, he reached into his shirt pocket to find his glasses, but they were gone. When he mentally replayed his earlier actions, he realized what happened; the glasses had slipped out of his pocket unnoticed and fallen into one of the crates, which he had nailed shut. His brand new glasses were heading for China! The Great Depression was at its height and Grandpa had six children. He had spent twenty dollars for those glasses that very morning. He was upset by the thought of having to buy another pair. "It's not fair," he told God, as he drove home in frustration. "I've been very faithful in giving of my time and money to your work, and now this."

Several months later, the director of the orphanage was on furlough in the United States. He wanted to visit all the churches that supported him in China, so he came one Sunday to speak at my grandfather's small church in Chicago. The missionary began by thanking the people for their faithfulness in supporting the orphanage. "But most of all," he said, "I must thank you for the glasses you sent last year. You see, the Communists had just swept through the orphanage, destroying everything, including my glasses. I was desperate. Even if I had the money, there was simply no way of replacing those glasses. Along with not being able to see well, I experienced headaches every day, so my coworkers and I were much in prayer about this. Then your crates arrived. When my staff removed the covers, they found a pair of glasses lying on top."

The missionary paused long enough to let his words sink in. Then, still gripped with the wonder of it all, he continued. "Folks, when I tried on the glasses, it was as though they had been custom-made just for me! I want to thank you for being a part of that." The people listened, happy for the miraculous glasses, but the missionary surely must have confused their church with another. There were no glasses on the list of items they sent overseas.

Sitting quietly in the back, with tears streaming down his face, an ordinary carpenter realized that by being faithful, the Master Carpenter had used him in an extraordinary way.

SURRENDER

TWO GOATS AND THE NARROW BRIDGE

Once there were two goats and a very narrow bridge over a river. One day a goat was crossing this bridge. Just at the middle of the bridge, he met another goat. There was no room for them to pass.

"Go back," said one goat to the other. "There is no room for both of us."

"Why should I go back?" said the other goat. "Better you go back."

"You must go back," said the first goat, "because I am stronger than you."

"You are not stronger than I," said the second goat.

"We will see about that," said the first goat, and he put down his horns to fight.

"Stop!" said the second goat. "If we fight, we shall both fall into the river and be drowned. I have a plan. I shall lie down and you may walk over me."

Then the wise one lay down on the bridge and the other goat walked over him. So they crossed the bridge comfortably and went on their ways.

TENACITY

THE ARMENIAN FATHER

In 1989 an 8.2 earthquake almost flattened Armenia, killing over 30,000 people in less than four minutes. After the earthquake, one father ran off to his son's school hoping to find him alive. The school building had totally caved in. Once he got over the shock, he remembered what he had always told his son: "You can always count on me. I will always be there for you." Even though it looked hopeless, be began to dig in the area where he thought his son might have been when the earthquake hit. Many people tried to discourage him, telling him he was wasting his time. He kept digging all by himself. He needed to find his son. He dug for eight hours with his hands. He was totally exhausted, could barely breathe because of the dirt and piles of debris. Tears kept filling his eyes. But he would not quit. Twelve hours. Twenty-four hours. Thirty-six hours. His arms could barely move anymore. Every muscle in his body screamed in pain. Then in the thirty-eighth hour, he moved one more stone and he heard his son's voice. He could hardly contain himself as he called him. His son immediately told the thirteen other classmates trapped with him that he knew his dad would come. The father told his son to grab his hand but the son replied, "Let's get everyone else out first, Dad."

KEEP YOUR EYES ON THE GOAL

On July 4, 1952, Florence Chadwick was on her way to becoming the first woman to swim the Catalina Channel. She had already conquered the English Channel. The world was watching. Chadwick fought dense fog, bone-chilling cold, and, many times, sharks. She was striving to reach the shore but every time she looked through her goggles, all she could see was the dense fog. Unable to see the shore, she gave up. Chadwick was disappointed when she found out that she was only half a mile from the coast. She quit, not because she was a quitter, but because she'd lost sight of her goal. The elements didn't stop her. She said, "I'm not making excuses. If only I had seen the land, I could have made it." Two months later, she went back and swam the Catalina Channel. This time, in spite of the bad weather, she had her goal in mind and not only accomplished it, but beat the men's record by two hours.[1]

THE STORY OF ERNEST SHACKLETON

Ernest Shackleton had a dream of crossing the Antarctic continent. He put up the following advertisement: "Men Wanted for Hazardous Journey. Small wages, bitter cold, long months of complete darkness, constant danger, safe return doubtful. Honor and recognition in case of success." Five thousand men responded. They wanted an adventure. In the end he chose twenty-seven men to accompany him aboard the ship, the "Endurance."

They left on August 9, 1914. They were thwarted when they were only one-day's sail and ninety-seven miles from their destination. The Endurance got stuck in the ice (now known as the Ronne Ice Shelf) off the Weddell Sea. A meteorologist reported that on February 14, 1915, the temperature dropped 40 degrees from +20 °F to –20 °F. The water froze, and the ship froze in with it.

Shackleton announced, "Abandon ship," on October 27, 1915 (eight months entrapped on ice). It was –15 °F. He bluntly told his crew, "What had happened, had happened. The ship and our stores have gone, so now we'll go home."

Shackleton changed, fanatically, from accomplishing his goal of Antarctic crossing, to bringing his men home safely. He decided to drag the one-ton loaded lifeboats for land—Elephant Island. It took them seven days to reach the island. Ultimately, in one of the most remarkable maritime crossings ever undertaken, Shackleton led a six-man crew in search of help across 800 nautical miles of the treacherous Southern Ocean to the island of South Georgia with only a twenty-three-foot whaleboat.

When he departed from Elephant Island towards the end of April 1916, Shackleton left twenty-two men behind, with his trusted second in command, Frank Wild. These men were left to patiently wait for the unknown day when Shackleton would hopefully return.

It took four attempts for Shackleton to finally make it back to Elephant Island to save the men left behind. Finally, on August 30, 1916, he made it back to rescue the entirety of his crew. Not a single life was lost![2]

THE TWO FROGS

One day, two frogs were enjoying the day in the barn when they accidentally fell into the farmer's bucket of cream, and they couldn't get out. The two frogs kept swimming around to keep from drowning, and every once in a while they would try to climb out, but this was becoming very tiring.

One frog kept saying, "This is useless, we should just give up." The other frog just ignored the comment and kept swimming. Finally, the pessimistic frog gave up and drowned. The other frog was sad at the loss of his friend, but he wasn't going to give up. He kept swimming and swimming, and, finally, the cream turned into butter and the frog simply climbed out.

This story shows that even if we stumble and others try to pull us down, we have to keep on swimming because, eventually, the problem (the cream) will turn into something better (the butter) and we'll make it out of problematic circumstance (the pail).

THE THIRSTY CROW

One hot day, a thirsty crow flew all over the fields looking for water. For a long time, she could not find any. She felt very weak, almost giving up hope.

Suddenly, she saw a water jug below her. She flew straight down to see if there was any water inside. Yes, she could see some water inside the jug!

The crow tried to push her head into the jug. Sadly, she found that the neck of the jug was too narrow. Then she tried to push the jug down for the water to flow out. She found that the jug was too heavy.

The crow thought hard for a while. Then looking around her, she saw some pebbles. She suddenly had a good idea. She started picking up the pebbles one by one, dropping each into the jug. As more and more pebbles filled the jug, the water level rose. Soon it was high enough for the crow to drink. Her plan had worked!

THE BUMBLEBEE

According to scientists, the bumblebee's body is too heavy and its wingspan too small to fly. Aerodynamically, the bumblebee cannot fly. The bumblebee doesn't know that, and it keeps flying. When you don't know your limitations, you go out and surprise yourself. In hindsight, you wonder if you had any limitations. The only limitations a person has are those that are self-imposed.

THE WILMA RUDOLPH STORY

Wilma Rudolph was born into a poor home in Tennessee. At age four, she had double pneumonia with scarlet fever, a deadly combination that weakens the immune system and leaves one vulnerable to polio. She contracted polio and was paralyzed her on the left side. She had to wear a brace, and the doctor said she would never put her foot on the earth again. Her mother encouraged her; she told Wilma that with God-given ability, persistence, and faith she could do anything she wanted. Wilma said, "I want to be the fastest woman on the track on this earth." At the age of nine, against the advice of the doctors, she removed the brace and took the first step the doctors had said she would never take. At the age of thirteen, she entered her first race and came in last. Then she entered her second and third and fourth race and still came in last, until a day came when she came in first. At the age of fifteen, she went to Tennessee State University where she met a coach by the name of Ed Temple. She told him, "I want to be the fastest woman on the track on this earth."

Temple said, "With your spirit nobody can stop you and besides, I will help you." The day came when she was at the Olympics where she was matched with the best of the best. Wilma was matched against a woman named Jutta Heine who had never been beaten. The first event was the hundred-meter race. Wilma beat Jutta Heine and won her first gold medal. The second event was the two-hundred-meter race and Wilma beat Jutta a second time and won her second gold medal. The third event was the four-hundred-meter relay and she was racing against Jutta one more time.

In the relay, the fastest person always runs the last lap and both Jutta and Wilma anchored their teams. The first three people ran and handed off the baton easily. When it came Wilma's turn, she dropped the baton. But when she saw Jutta shoot up at the other end; she picked the baton, ran like a machine, beat Jutta a third time, and won her third gold medal. It became history: A paralytic woman became the fastest woman on this earth at the 1960 Olympics.

SPARKY
MELANIE JOHNSON

When you feel yourself slipping, remember Sparky. School was all but impossible for Sparky. He failed every subject in the eighth grade. He flunked physics, Latin, algebra, and English in high school. He didn't do much better in sports. Although he did manage to make the school golf team, he promptly lost the only important match of the year. There was a consolation match and he lost that, too. Throughout his youth, Sparky was awkward socially. He was not actually disliked by the other students; he wasn't considered consequential enough for that! He was astonished if a classmate ever said "hello" to him outside school hours. He never found out how he would have fared as a "date." In high school, Sparky never once asked a girl out. He was too afraid of being rejected. Sparky was a loser. He, his classmates, and everyone else knew it, so Sparky simply accepted it.

One thing was important to Sparky: drawing. He was proud of his own artwork. Of course, no one else appreciated it. In his senior year in high school, he submitted some cartoons to the editors of his yearbook. His cartoons were turned down. Despite this particularly painful rejection, Sparky had found his passion. Upon graduating from high school, he wrote a letter to Walt Disney Studios. They requested he send samples of his artwork. The studio suggested the subject matter for a cartoon. Sparky drew the proposed cartoon. He spent a great deal of time on it and on the other drawings. Eventually, the reply from the Disney Studios came. He had been rejected once again. Another loss for the loser.

Sparky wrote his own autobiography in cartoons. He described his childhood self, a little-boy loser and chronic underachiever. He was the little cartoon boy whose kite would never fly, who never succeeded in kicking the football, and who became the most famous cartoon character of all, Charlie Brown! Sparky, the boy who failed every subject in the eighth grade and whose work was rejected again and again was Charles Schulz.[3] Charles Schulz persevered. He succeeded beyond his wildest imagination. He earned and deserved that success. He had failed at everything else he had tried. He endured rejection. It took a lot of trial and error to learn what it was that he was supposed to do. He never quit. Because Charles Schulz persevered, the world is richer.

KENTUCKY FRIED TENACITY

Colonel Sanders, at age sixty-five, with a beat-up car and a $100 check from Social Security, realized he had to do something. He remembered his mother's chicken recipe and went out selling, but it wasn't easy. It is estimated that he had knocked on more than a thousand doors before he got his first order.[4] How many of us would quit after three tries, ten tries, a hundred tries, and then we say we tried as hard as we could?

THE FARMER'S DONKEY

One day a farmer's donkey fell down a well. The animal cried piteously for hours as the farmer tried to figure out what to do. Finally, he decided the animal was old and the well needed to be covered up anyway; it just wasn't worth the effort to retrieve the donkey.

He invited all his neighbors to come and help him. They all grabbed shovels and began to shovel dirt into the well. At first, the donkey realized what was happening and cried horribly. Then, to everyone's amazement, he quieted down.

A few shovel loads later, the farmer finally looked down the well. He was astonished at what he saw. With each shovel of dirt that hit his back, the donkey was doing something amazing. He would shake it off and take a step up. As the farmer's neighbors continued to shovel dirt on top of the animal, he would shake it off and take a step up.

Soon, everyone was amazed as the donkey stepped up over the edge of the well, and happily trotted off!

Life is going to shovel dirt on you, all kinds of dirt. The trick to getting out of the well is to shake it off and take a step up. Each of our troubles is a step up. We can get out of the deepest wells of trouble by not stopping and never giving up! Shake it off and take a step up.

UNDERSTANDING

THE SIX BLIND MEN AND THE ELEPHANT
JOHN GODFREY SAXE

There are various versions of the story of the blind men and the elephant, a legend that appears in different cultures—notably China, Africa, and India, and the tale dates back thousands of years. Some versions of the story feature three blind men, others five or six, but the message is always the same. Here's a story of the six blind men and the elephant.

Six blind men were discussing exactly what they believed an elephant to be, since each had heard how strange the creature was, and yet none had ever experienced one before. The blind men agreed to find an elephant and discover what the animal was really like.

It didn't take them long to find an elephant at a nearby market. The first blind man approached the beast and felt the animal's firm flat side. "It seems to me that the elephant is like a wall," he said to his friends.

The second blind man reached out and touched one of the elephant's tusks. "No, this is round and smooth and sharp. The elephant is like a spear."

Intrigued, the third blind man stepped up to the elephant and touched its trunk. "Well, I can't agree with either of you; I feel a squirming writhing thing. Surely the elephant is like a snake."

The fourth blind man was, of course, by now quite puzzled. He reached out and felt the elephant's leg. "You are all talking complete nonsense," he said, "because clearly the elephant is like a tree."

Utterly confused, the fifth blind man stepped forward and grabbed one of the elephant's ears. "You must all be mad. An elephant is like a fan."

Duly, the sixth man approached, and holding the beast's tail, disagreed again. "It's nothing like any of your descriptions. The elephant is like a rope."

All six blind men continued to argue, based on their own particular experiences, as to what they thought an elephant was like. It was an argument they were never able to resolve. Each of them was concerned only with their own idea. None of them had the full picture and none understood any of the other's points of view. Each man experienced the elephant as something quite different, and while in part each blind man was right, none was wholly correct.[1]

There is never just one way to look at something—there are always different perspectives, meanings, and perceptions, depending on who is looking.

POISE

A SMILE

Those who fight the good fight and win need to be brave only once.
Those who lose must show courage twice.
Therefore, we must steel ourselves for harder things than triumph.
Let others cheer the winning man,
I hold one worthwhile.
It is he who does the best he can,
Then loses with a smile.
Beaten he is, but not to stay down with the rank and file;
That man will win some other day who loses with a smile.[1]

HASTE MAKES WASTE

A woman had a pet mongoose. It was very faithful. One day she went to the market, leaving her baby in the care of the mongoose. At that time, a big cobra entered the house. The mongoose killed it after a long and fierce fight. When the woman came back, she saw the mongoose lying at the entrance. She noticed its blood-covered mouth. In her haste the woman thought that the mongoose had killed her baby. In a moment of sudden fury, the woman threw the water pot on the mongoose and killed it. Alas! When she entered the house, she was filled with remorse. Her baby was playing cheerfully. Nearby a big cobra lay dead. The woman shed tears of grief, fondling the carcass of the mongoose.

THE SHOEBOX

There was once a man and a woman who had been married for more than sixty years. They had shared everything. They had talked about everything.

They had kept no secrets from each other except that the little old woman had a shoebox in the top of her closet. She had cautioned her husband never to open or ask her about it. For all the years, he had not thought about the box, but one day the little old woman got very sick and the doctor said she would not recover. In trying to sort out their affairs, the little old man took down the shoebox and took it to his wife's bedside. She agreed that it was time for him to know what was in the box. When he opened it, he found two crocheted doilies and a stack of money totaling $25,000. He asked her about the contents. "When we were to be married," she said, "my grandmother told me the secret of a happy marriage was to never argue. She told me that if I ever got angry with you, I should just keep quiet and crochet a doily." The little old man was so moved that he had to fight back tears. Only two precious doilies were in the box. She had only been angry with him two times in all those years of living and loving. He almost burst with happiness.

"Honey," he said, "that explains the doilies, but what about all of this money? Where did it come from?"

"Oh," she said, "that's the money I made from selling doilies."

JUGGLE BALLS

Imagine life as a game in which you are juggling some five balls in the air. You name them: work, family, health, friends, and spirit. You're keeping all of these in the air. You will soon understand that work is a rubber ball. If you drop it, it will bounce back. However, the other four balls, family, health, friends, and spirit, are made of glass. If you drop one of these, they will be irrevocably scuffed, marked, nicked, damaged, or even shattered. They will never be the same. You must understand that and strive for balance in your life. How?

- Don't undermine your worth by comparing yourself with others. It is because we are different that each of us is special.
- Don't set your goals by what other people deem important. Only you know what is best for you.
- Don't take for granted the things closest to your heart. Cling to them as you would your life, for without them, life is meaningless.
- Don't let your life slip through your fingers by living in the past or for the future. By living your life one day at a time, you live ALL the days of your life.

- Don't give up when you still have something to give. Nothing is really over until the moment you stop trying.
- Don't be afraid to admit that you are less than perfect. It is this fragile thread that binds us each together.
- Don't be afraid to encounter risks. It is by taking chances that we learn how to be brave.
- Don't shut love out of your life by saying it's impossible to find. The quickest way to receive love is to give; the fastest way to lose love is to hold it too tightly; and the best way to keep love is to give it wings.
- Don't run through life so fast that you forget not only where you've been, but also where you are going.
- Don't forget that a person's greatest emotional need is to feel appreciated.
- Don't be afraid to learn. Knowledge is weightless, a treasure you can always carry easily.
- Don't use time or words carelessly. Neither can be retrieved. Life is not a race, but a journey to be savored each step of the way.

PRUDENCE

ONE NUT AND TWO BOYS

Two little boys were playing together. One little boy saw a nut on the ground. Before he could pick it up the other boy took it. The first boy demanded, "Give me the nut. It's mine. I saw it first."

The other boy replied, "It's mine. I took it." This led to a quarrel between these two little boys. Just then a tall boy came their way. Upon seeing the quarrel between the boys, he said, "Give me the nut and I'll settle your quarrel." He split the nut into two parts. He took out the fruit seed. He gave half of the shell to one boy and the second half to the other boy. He put the fruit seed into his mouth and said, "This is for settling your quarrel."

Moral: When two people quarrel, someone else always gains.

THE GOOSE AND THE GOLDEN EGGS
AESOP

Once upon a time, a man and his wife had the good fortune to have a goose that laid a golden egg every day. Lucky though they were, they soon began to think they were not getting rich fast enough.

They imagined that if the bird must be able to lay golden eggs, its insides must be made of gold. They thought that if they could get all that precious metal at once, they would get mighty rich very soon. The man and his wife decided to kill the bird.

However, upon cutting the goose open, they were shocked to find that its innards were like that of any other goose! The moral of the story is: Think before you act.

THE ANT AND THE GRASSHOPPER
AESOP

In a field one summer's day, a grasshopper was hopping about, chirping and singing to its heart's content. An ant passed by, bearing along with great toil an ear of corn he was taking to the nest.

"Why not come and chat with me," said the grasshopper, "instead of toiling and moiling in that way?"

"I am helping to lay up food for the winter," said the ant, "and I recommend you to do the same."

"Why bother about winter?" said the grasshopper; we have plenty of food at present."

The ant went on its way and continued its toil. When the winter came, the grasshopper had no food and found itself dying of hunger. The ants, however, every day distributed corn and grain from the stores they had collected in the summer.

Then the grasshopper knew: It is best to prepare for the days of necessity.

JUSTICE

THE FATHER, HIS SON, AND THEIR DONKEY
AESOP

A father and his son were taking their donkey to a neighboring town to sell him. They had not gone far when they met with a group of women sitting near a well, talking and laughing. "Look there," cried one of them, "Did you ever see such an injustice, a father and his son trudging along the road on foot when they could be riding on their donkey?'

The old man, hearing this, quickly made his son get up on the donkey, and continued to walk along merrily by his side. Presently they came up to a group of old men along the side of the road arguing. "There," said one of them. "It proves what I was saying. Old people get no respect these days. Do you see that lazy boy riding while his old father has to walk? What an injustice! Get down off that donkey, you lazy boy, and let the old man rest his weary limbs." Upon hearing that, the old man made his son get down off the donkey and got up himself.

With the father on the donkey and the boy trying to keep pace next to them, they had not proceeded far when they met a group of women and children. "Why, you lazy old man," cried several tongues at once, "how can you ride upon the beast, while that poor little lad can hardly keep pace with you?" The good-natured father immediately lifted up his son up behind him, and they both rode on the donkey.

They had now almost reached the town when they came upon another man walking alone. "Pray, honest friend," said the man, "does that donkey belong to you?"

"Yes," replied the father.

"I can hardly believe that," said the man, "by the way you are unjustly making him carry both of you. Why, you two fellows are better able to carry the donkey, than the donkey carry you."

"Anything to please you," said the father. "We can but try." So with his son, they tied the legs of the donkey together and with the help of a long pole started to carry the donkey on their shoulders.

Soon they came to a bridge near the entrance to the town. The entertaining sight of the father and his son carrying the donkey on a long pole brought the townspeople near the bridge to laugh aloud. They made so much noise that the donkey became scared and as he struggled to get loose from the pole he broke the ropes and tumbled off the bridge and into the river.

Upon this, the father, frustrated, embarrassed, and ashamed, made his way home with his son, convinced that by trying to serve justice for everybody, he had pleased nobody, and lost his ass in the bargain.

FORTITUDE

THE BUTTERFLY

A man found butterfly cocoon. One day a small opening appeared. He sat and watched the butterfly for several hours as it struggled to force its body through that little hole. Then it seemed to stop making any progress. It appeared as if it had gotten as far as it could, and it could go no further.

The man decided to help the butterfly. He took a pair of scissors and snipped off the remaining bit of the cocoon. The butterfly then emerged easily, but it had a swollen body and small, shriveled wings.

The man continued to watch the butterfly because he expected that at any moment, the wings would enlarge and expand to be able to support the body, which would contract in size in time. Neither happened! In fact, the butterfly spent the rest of its life crawling around with a swollen body and shriveled wings. It never was able to fly.

What the man in his kindness and haste did not understand was that the restricting cocoon and the struggle required for the butterfly to get through the tiny opening were God's way of forcing fluid from the body of the butterfly into its wings so that it would be ready for flight once it achieved its freedom from the cocoon.

Sometimes struggles are exactly what we need in our lives. If we went through life without any obstacles, we would be crippled. We would not be as strong as what we could have been. We could never fly!

THE STORY OF KYLE MAYNARD

Kyle Maynard was born with deformed arms and legs, but that never stopped him from becoming a Division 1 collegiate wrestler at the University of Georgia. He has no arms beyond two rounded stumps and no legs apart from a pair of short appendages with deformed feet. Growing up, Kyle would watch other kids grip crayons between thumb and fingers, so he quickly taught himself to clutch objects between his two shortened but highly sensitive biceps. It is the same technique he uses today to wrangle French fries, pop open acne medicine packages and manipulate an itty-bitty cell phone. Want more? He also can type fifty words a minute. Nothing has ever come easy for Kyle but he is a man of determination. He lost his first thirty-five wrestling matches, but he never stopped improving. When he was a senior in high school, he had a record of thirty-five wins and sixteen losses. He won ESPN's ESPY Award for best athlete with a disability and a Courage Award from the World Sports Humanitarian Hall of Fame. He topped that off with a 3.7 grade point average while finishing twelfth at the 103-pound weight class at the National High School Wrestling Championships. The next time you want to feel sorry for yourself or give in and give up when the going gets tough, think of Kyle. Kyle was and is intent on being the absolute best he can be. He does not listen when other people tell him that he cannot accomplish something. He sets his mind to it and he gives it his all.

No excuses, no complaints—just sheer determination. Kyle is a man with an iron will who does not listen to his feelings when they come whining. He listens to his will and has the heart to follow through.

DR. LIVINGSTON I PRESUME

While he was on a missionary trip in remote Africa, Dr. David Livingston was approached by an organization in England that wanted to send him some assistance. The leader of the organization wrote to him, asking, "Have you found a good road to where you are? If so, we want to send some men to join you on this mission."

Dr. Livingston wrote back, "If you only have men who will come if they know there is a good road, I don't want them. I want men who will come even if there is no road at all."[1]

TEMPERANCE

GHENGIS KAHN AND HIS HAWK
JAMES BALDWIN

One morning, when he was home from the wars, the king rode out into the woods to have a day's sport. Many of his friends were with him. They rode out in good spirits, carrying their bows and arrows. Behind them came the servants with the hounds. It was a merry hunting party. The woods rang with their shouts and laughter. They expected to carry much game home in the evening.

On the king's wrist sat his favorite hawk, for in those days hawks were trained to hunt. At a word from their master the hawk would fly high up into the air, and look around for prey. If it chanced to see a deer or a rabbit, it would swoop down upon it swift as any arrow.

All day long Genghis Khan and his huntsmen rode through the woods. They did not find as much game as they expected. Toward evening, they started for home. The king had often ridden through the woods, and he knew all the paths. While the rest of the party took the nearest way, he went by a longer road through a valley between two mountains. The day had been warm, and the king was very thirsty. His pet hawk had left his wrist and flown away. It would find its way home.

The king rode slowly along. He had once seen a spring of clear water near this pathway. If he could only find it now! But the hot days of summer had dried up all the mountain brooks. At last, to his joy, he saw some water trickling down over the edge of a rock. He knew that there was a spring farther up. In the wet season, a swift stream of water always poured down here; but now it came only one drop at a time. The king leaped from his horse. He took a little silver cup from his hunting bag. He held it so as to catch the slowly falling drops.

It took a long time to fill the cup; and the king was so thirsty that he could hardly wait. At last it was nearly full. He put the cup to his lips, and was about to drink. All at once, there was a whirring sound in the air and the cup was knocked from his hands. The water spilled upon the ground. The king looked up to see who had done this thing. It was his pet hawk. The hawk flew back and forth a few times, and then alighted among the rocks by the spring.

The king picked up the cup, and again held it to catch the trickling drops. This time he did not wait so long. When the cup was half full, he lifted it toward his mouth. But before it had touched his lips, the hawk swooped down again, and knocked it from his hands. Now the king began to grow angry. He tried again, and for the third time the hawk kept him from drinking.

The king was now very angry indeed. "How do you dare to act so?" he cried. "If I had you in my hands, I would wring your neck!" Then he filled the cup again. Before he tried to drink, he drew his sword.

"Now, Sir Hawk," he said, "This is the last time." He had hardly spoken before the hawk swooped down and knocked the cup from his hand. The king was looking for this. With a quick sweep of the sword, he struck the bird as it passed. The next moment the poor hawk laid bleeding and dying at its master's feet.

"That is what you get for your pains," said Genghis Khan. When he looked for his cup, he found that it had fallen between two rocks, where he could not reach it. "At any rate, I will have a drink from that spring," he said to himself.

With that, he began to climb the steep bank to the place from which the water trickled. It was hard work, and the higher he climbed, the thirstier he became. At last he reached the place. There indeed was a pool of water; but what was that lying in the pool, and almost filling it? It was a huge, dead snake of the most poisonous kind.

The king stopped. He forgot his thirst. He thought only of the poor dead bird lying on the ground below him. "The hawk saved my life!" he cried, "and how did I repay him? He was my best friend, and I have killed him."

He clambered down the bank. He took up the bird gently, and laid it in his hunting bag. Then he mounted his horse and rode swiftly home. He said to himself, "I have learned a sad lesson today, and that is, never to do anything in anger."[1]

THE GREEDY MOUSE

A greedy mouse saw a basket full of corn. He wanted to eat it, so he made a small hole in the basket. He squeezed in through the hole. He ate a lot of corn. He felt full. He was very happy.

Now he wanted to come out. He tried to come out through the small hole. He could not. His belly was full. He tried again. It was of no use.

The mouse started crying. A rabbit was passing by. It heard the mouse's cry and asked, "Why are you crying, my friend?"

The mouse explained, "I made a small hole and came into the basket. Now I am not able to get out through that hole."

The rabbit said, "It is because you ate too much. Wait 'til your belly shrinks." The rabbit laughed and went away.

The mouse fell asleep in the basket. The next morning, his belly had shrunk. The mouse wanted to eat some corn—so he ate and ate. His belly was full once again. He thought, *Oh! Now I will go out tomorrow.*

The cat was the next passerby. He smelled the mouse in the basket. He lifted its lid. He ate the mouse.

FAITH

THE BURNING HUT

The only survivor of a shipwreck washed up on a small, uninhabited island. He prayed feverishly for God to rescue him, and every day he scanned the horizon for help, but none seemed forthcoming. Exhausted, he eventually managed to build a little hut out of driftwood to protect him from the elements, and create a place where he could store his few possessions. One day, after scavenging for food, he arrived home to find his little hut in flames, the smoke rolling up to the sky. The worst had happened; everything was lost. He was stung with grief and anger. "God, how could you do this to me!" he cried.

Early the next day, however, he was awakened by the sound of a ship approaching the island. It had come to rescue him. "How did you know I was here?" asked the weary man.

"We saw your smoke signal," they replied.

It is easy to get discouraged when things are going badly. But we shouldn't lose heart, because God is at work in our lives, even in the midst of pain and suffering.

Remember next time your little hut is burning to the ground, it may just be a smoke signal that summons the grace of God.

RECOGNIZING FAITH

A flood was threatening a small town, and everyone was leaving for safety except one man who said, "God will save me. I have faith." As the water level rose a jeep came to rescue him. The man refused, saying, "God will save me. I have faith." As the water level rose further, he went up to the second story, and a boat came to help him. Again he refused to go, saying, "God will save me. I have faith." The water kept rising and the man climbed on to the roof. A helicopter came to rescue him, but he said, "God will save me. I have faith." Well, finally he drowned. When he reached his Maker he angrily questioned, "I had complete faith in you. Why did you ignore my prayers and let me drown?" The Lord replied, "Who do you think sent you the jeep, the boat, and the helicopter?"

THE ROPE

The night fell heavy in the heights of the mountains and the man could not see anything. All was black. Zero visibility, the moon and the stars covered by the clouds. As he was climbing, only a few feet from the top of the mountain, he slipped and fell into the air, falling at great speed. He could only see black spots as he went down, and the terrible sensation of being sucked by gravity.

He kept falling, and in the moments of great fear, it came to his mind all the good and bad episodes of his life. He was thinking now about how close death was. All of a sudden he felt the rope tied to his waist pull him very hard. His body was hanging in the air.

Only the rope was holding him, and in that moment of stillness he had no other choice other to scream, "Help me God."

All of a sudden a deep voice coming from the sky answered, "What do you want me to do?"

"Save me, God."

"Do you really think I can save you?"

"Of course. I have faith that you can."

"Then cut the rope tied to your waist."

There was a moment of silence and the man decided to hold onto the rope with all his strength. The rescue team tells that the next day they found a climber dead and frozen, his body hanging from a rope, his hands holding tightly to it. He was only one foot away from the ground.

HOPE

ONE STARFISH

A vacationing businessman was walking along a beach when he saw a young boy. Along the shore were many starfish that had been washed up by the tide and were sure to die before the tide returned. The boy walked slowly along the shore and occasionally reached down and tossed a beached starfish back into the ocean. The businessman, hoping to teach the boy a little lesson in common sense and futility, walked up to the boy and said, "I have been watching what you are doing, son. You have a good heart, and I know you mean well, but do you realize how many beaches there are around here and how many starfish are dying on every beach every day? Surely, such an industrious and kindhearted boy such as yourself could find something better to do with your time. Do you really think that what you are doing is going to make a difference?"

The boy looked up at the man, and then he looked down at a starfish by his feet. He picked up the starfish, and as he gently tossed it back into the ocean, he said, "It makes a difference to that one."

THE CRACKED POT

A water bearer in India had two large pots, one hung on each end of a pole that he carried across his neck. One of the pots had a crack in it, so while the other pot was perfect and always delivered a full portion of water at the end of the long walk from the stream to the master's house, the cracked pot arrived only half full.

For a full two years this went on daily, with the bearer delivering only one-and-a-half pots full of water to his master's house. Of course, the perfect pot was proud of its accomplishments. It fulfilled perfectly that for which it was made. But the poor cracked pot was ashamed of its own imperfection. It was miserable that it was able to accomplish only half of what it had been made to do. After two years of what it perceived to be a bitter failure, it spoke to the water bearer one day by the stream.

"I am ashamed of myself, and I want to apologize to you."

"Why?" asked the bearer. "What are you ashamed of?"

"I have been able, for these past two years, to deliver only half my load because this crack in my side causes water to leak out all the way back to your master's house. Because of my flaws, you have to do all of this work, and you don't get full value from your efforts."

The water bearer felt sorry for the old cracked pot, and in his compassion he said, "As we return to the master's house, I want you to notice the beautiful flowers along the path."

Indeed, as they went up the hill, the old cracked pot took notice of the sun warming the beautiful wild flowers on the side of the path, and this cheered it some. But at the end of the trail, it still felt bad because it had leaked out half of its load, and so again it apologized to the bearer for its failure.

The bearer said to the pot, "Did you notice that there were flowers only on your side of your path, but not on the other pot's side? That's because I have always known about your flaw, and I took advantage of it. I planted flower seeds on your side of the path, and every day while we walk back from the stream, you've watered them. For two years, I have been able to pick these beautiful flowers to decorate my master's table. Without you being just the way you are, he would not have this beauty to grace his house."

THE FROGS

A group of frogs was traveling through the woods, and two of them fell into a deep pit. All the other frogs gathered around the pit. When they saw how deep the pit was, they told the two frogs that they were as good as dead. The two frogs ignored the comments and tried to jump out of the pit with all of their might. The other frogs kept telling them to stop, that they were as good as dead. Finally, one of the frogs took heed to what the other frogs were saying and gave up. He fell down and died. The other frog continued to jump as hard as he could. Once again, the crowd of frogs yelled at him to stop the pain and just die. He jumped even harder and finally made it out. When he got out, the other frogs said, "Did you not hear us?" The frog explained to them that he was deaf. He thought they were encouraging him the entire time.

THE MIRACLE ON ICE

During the 1980 Olympic Winter Games in Lake Placid, New York, a team of amateur and collegiate ice hockey players from the United States, some of whom had signed contracts to play in the National Hockey League, beat the long-dominant and heavily favored Soviet Union. The game was dubbed "The Miracle on Ice."

The US team entered the competition seeded seventh in the final round of twelve teams that qualified for the Lake Placid Olympics; the Soviet Union was the favorite. A year earlier, the Soviet national team had routed the NHL all-stars 6-0 to win the Challenge Cup. Two weeks before the Olympic match-up, the two Olympic teams met for an exhibition match in order to practice for the upcoming competition. The Soviet Union won 10-3. In Olympic group play, the United States surprised many observers with their physical, cohesive play, starting with a 2-2 tie against Sweden and followed by a stunning 7-3 victory against a strong team from Czechoslovakia. Finishing with four wins and one draw, the US team advanced to the medal round. In the other group, the Soviets stormed through their opposition undefeated, demolishing their opponents: Japan 16-0, the Netherlands 17-4, and Poland 8-1. Sweden and Finland also qualified for the medal round.

Can you imagine preparing to play a team that previously beat you 10-3 and shut out a team of NHL all-stars 6-0? During the game, the Soviets had thirty-nine shots on goal, while the Americans had only sixteen. It was tied 2-2 at the end of the first period, then the Soviet Union went ahead 3-2 at the end of the second period. With ten minutes left to play, the US made it 4-3. They held on for the victory. They held on for a miracle. The United States went on to win the gold medal by beating Finland in their final game.

KEEP YOUR FORK, THE BEST IS YET TO COME
ROGER WILLIAM THOMAS

There was a woman who had been diagnosed with a terminal illness and was given three months to live. As she began getting her things "'in order," she called her pastor and asked him to come to her house to discuss certain aspects of her final wishes. She told him which songs she wanted sung at the service, what scriptures she wanted read, and what dress she wanted to be buried in. She also requested to be buried with her favorite Bible in her left hand. Everything was in order and as the pastor was preparing to leave, the woman suddenly remembered one final request that was very important to her.

"Please Pastor, just one more thing," she said excitedly.

"Sure, what is it?" Came the pastor's reply.

"This is very important to me," the woman continued. "I want to be buried holding a fork in my right hand."

The pastor gazed at the woman, at a loss for words.

"That surprises you, doesn't it?" the woman asked.

The pastor replied, "Well to be quite honest, I am puzzled by the request."

The woman explained. "You see, Pastor, in all my years of attending church socials and potluck dinners, I remember that when the dishes were being cleared after the main course, someone would inevitably lean over to me and say, 'Keep your fork.' It was my favorite part of the meal because I knew that something better was coming, like velvety chocolate cake or deep-dish apple pie. Something wonderful to end the meal!"

The pastor listened intently and a smile came upon his face. The woman continued, "So, I just want people to see me there with a fork in my hand and I want them to wonder, 'What's with the fork'... then I want you to tell them, 'Keep your fork ... the best is yet to come.'"

The pastor's eyes welled up with tears of joy as he hugged the woman good-bye. He knew that this would be one of the last times that he would see her before her death. He also knew that the woman had a better grasp of Heaven than he did.

She knew and trusted that the best was yet to come. At the funeral everyone who walked by the woman's casket saw her wearing a beautiful dress with her favorite Bible held in her left hand and a fork held in her right hand.

Over and over the pastor heard people ask the question, "Why is she holding a fork?" and his smile began to get larger and brighter each time. During his message, the pastor told the people about the conversation he had with the woman shortly before she died. He explained the fork and what it symbolized to her. The pastor told everyone how he could not stop thinking about the fork and how he hoped that they would not be able to stop thinking about it either.

So the next time you reach for your fork, let it remind you, oh so gently, that the best is yet to come.[1]

LOVE

LOVE MAKES A DIFFERENCE

Helen Keller (1880–1968) was the first deaf-blind person to achieve a bachelor of arts degree, and her amazing life still inspires many. Queen Victoria of England reportedly asked Keller, "How do you account for your remarkable accomplishment in life…that even though you are both blind and deaf, you have accomplished so much?"

Ms. Keller responded with a now-famous tribute to her dedicated teacher: "If it had not been for Anne Sullivan, the name Helen Keller would have remained unknown."

Helen's future teacher, nearly sightless herself, was declared hopelessly insane as a child because she fluctuated between ignoring those around her and viciously attacking them. Nicknamed "Little Annie", she was even locked in the basement of a mental institution.

But her life was altered by an elderly nurse who believed that she could make a difference simply by showing love to Little Annie. Despite the fact that Little Annie ignored her completely, the determined nurse visited every day. She delivered cookies and showered her with words of love and encouragement. Remarkably, Little Annie did begin to respond, behaving more gently and showing the capacity to be loving toward others. As her anger and hostility gradually melted away, her surprised doctors moved her upstairs. Finally, Little Annie—once declared a hopeless case—was released from the institution altogether.

Anne Sullivan drew on her childhood struggles and the love shown by that nurse to become an empathetic young woman. She was able to see hope and potential in Helen Keller where others could not. Through consistent love, companionship, and discipline, Anne was able to break into Helen's isolated world, teaching her to communicate and inspiring her to greatness.

Many years later, when Helen Keller responded to Queen Victoria's question, she credited Anne Sullivan with her success. Yet Anne Sullivan would not have had the capacity to love and motivate Helen to greatness if it hadn't been for the love of an old nurse, which had transformed her from an incommunicative child into a caring teacher.

The power of love is far-reaching and eternal. The influence of one person with a compassionate heart can not only change another person's life; it can change history.

A GIFT OF LOVE

"Can I see my baby?" the happy new mother asked. When the bundle was nestled in her arms, she moved the fold of cloth to look upon his tiny face. She gasped. The doctor turned quickly and looked out the tall hospital window. The baby had been born without ears. Time proved that the baby's hearing was perfect. It was only his appearance that was marred. When he rushed home from school one day and flung himself into his mother's arms, she sighed, knowing that his life was to be a succession of heartbreaks.

He blurted out the tragedy. "A boy, a big boy, called me a freak."

The boy grew up, handsome for his misfortune. A favorite with his fellow students, he might have been class president, but for his look. He developed a gift, a talent for literature and music. "You might mingle with other young people," his mother reproved him, but felt a kindness in her heart.

The boy's father had a session with the family physician. Could nothing be done? "I believe I could graft on a pair of outer ears, if they could be procured," the doctor decided. The search began for a person who would make such a sacrifice for the young man. Two years went by.

Then the father said, "You are going to the hospital, son. Mother and I have found someone who will donate the ears you need. But it's a secret."

The operation was a brilliant success, and a new person emerged. His talents blossomed into genius and school and college became a series of triumphs. Later he married and entered the diplomatic service. "But

I must know!" He urged his father. "Who gave so much for me? I could never do enough for him."

"I do not believe you could," said the father, "but the agreement was that you are not to know...not yet." For years, the profound secret was kept, but eventually the day came—one of the darkest days that a son could ever pass through. He stood with his father over his mother's casket. Slowly, tenderly, the father stretched forth a hand and raised the thick, reddish-brown hair to reveal...the mother had no outer ears.

"Mother said she was glad she never let her hair be cut," he whispered gently. "And nobody ever thought mother less beautiful, did they?"

Real beauty lies not in the physical appearance, but in the heart. Real treasure lies not in what can be seen, but what cannot be seen. Real love lies less in what is done and known, than in what that is done, and not known.

THE BEST MEDICINE

During the first two decades of the twentieth century, a great number of babies under one year of age wasted away in hospitals and children's institutions and died from unknown causes. In some institutions it was customary to enter the condition of all seriously sick infants as "hopeless" on admission cards.

Among the doctors confronted with infant mortality daily was Dr. Fritz Talbot of the Children's Clinic in Dusseldorf. Dr. Talbot had uncommon success in dealing with sick children. For many years, as he made his rounds, he would be followed from ward to ward by groups of interns seeking new ways of handling children's diseases. One such intern was Dr. Joseph Brennermann, who told this story.

"Many times we would come across a child for whom everything had failed. For some reason the child was hopelessly wasting away. When this would happen, Dr. Talbot would take the child's chart and scrawl some indecipherable prescription. In most of the cases, the magic formula took effect and the child began to prosper. My curiosity was aroused and I wondered if the famous doctor had developed some new type of wonder drug.

"One day, after rounds, I returned to the ward and tried to decipher Dr. Talbot's scrawl. I had no luck, and so I turned to the head nurse and asked her what the prescription was.

"Old Anna," she said. Then she pointed to a grandmotherly woman seated in a large rocker with a baby on her lap. The nurse continued. "Whenever we have a baby for whom everything we do fails, we turn the child over to Old Anna. She has more success than all the doctors and nurses in this institution combined.' "[1]

COMING HOME AFTER A HARD DAY'S WORK

A man came home from work late again, tired and irritated, to find his five-year-old son waiting for him at the door. "Daddy, can I ask a question?"

"Yeah, sure, what is it?"

"Daddy, how much money do you make an hour?"

"That's none of your business! What makes you ask such a thing?"

The little boy pleaded. "I just want to know. Please tell me, how much do you make an hour?"

"If I tell you, will you leave me alone? Okay, I make twenty dollars an hour."

"Oh," the little boy replied, head bowed down. Looking up, he said, "Daddy, may I borrow ten dollars, please?"

The father was furious. "If the only reason you wanted to know how much money I make is so you can borrow some to buy a silly toy or some other nonsense, then you march yourself straight to your room and go to bed. Think about why you are being so selfish. I work long, hard hours every day and don't have time for such childish games."

The little boy quietly went to his room and shut the door. The man sat down and stewed about the little boy's questioning. How dare he ask such questions only to get some money!

After an hour or so, the man had calmed down and started to think he might have been a little hard on his son, thinking perhaps he really needed to buy something with those ten dollars. And besides, he really didn't ask for money often. The man went to the door of the little boy's room and opened the door. "Are you asleep, son?" he asked.

"No, Daddy, I'm awake," replied the boy.

"I've been thinking, maybe I was too hard on you earlier," said the man. "It's been a long day, and I took my aggravation out on you. Here's that ten dollars you asked for."

The little boy sat straight up, beaming. "Oh, thank you, Daddy!" he yelled. Then, reaching under his pillow, he pulled out some more crumpled-up bills. The man, seeing that the boy already had money, became angry again. The little boy slowly counted out his money, then looked up at the man.

The father grumbled. "Why did you want more money if you already had some?"

"Because I didn't have enough, but now I do," the little boy replied. "Daddy, I have twenty dollars now. Can I buy an hour of your time to play catch with me?"

BIG WILLY
NANCY BOUCHARD

He stood six-foot, nine inches tall and weighed in at 310 pounds. Rumor had it that he'd killed a man with his bare hands—just squeezed the life out of him. It was the kind of reputation that gained respect in the rough city where we grew up. At fifteen, Willy was already a legend.

Willy and I played together since we both wore diapers, although we were the unlikeliest of pairs. He was a massive black giant and I was a pudgy little redhead. We both worked at the factory in town—I in the office, Willy on the dock. Even the hardened men who worked alongside Willy feared him.

He saw me home safely from work. I kept his secret that each night, instead of cruising the city streets, beating people up, he went home and lovingly lifted his elderly grandmother out of the chair where she was confined and place her in bed. He would read to her until she fell asleep, and in the morning, he would comb her thin, gray hair, dress her in the beautiful nightgowns he bought with the money he made at the can company, and place her back in the chair.

Willy had lost both his parents to drugs, and it was just the two of them now. He took care of her, and she gave him a reason to stay clean. Of course, there wasn't an ounce of truth to the rumors, but Willy never said otherwise. He just let everyone believe what they believed, and although everyone wrote him off as just another street hood, no one hassled him either.

One day, in Western Civilization class, our teacher read aloud an excerpt from Machiavelli's *The Prince*. "Since love and fear cannot exist together, if we must choose between them, it is far safer to be feared than loved." I looked at Willy and winked. "That's you," I mouthed. He just smiled.

The next day, I lingered a few minutes longer than usual at school and Willy went on without me. Just around the corner from the can company, fire trucks lined the street and a thick blanket of smoke covered the sky. A small child lay wrapped in a familiar red-and-black checkered flannel shirt, held by a tearful woman. She was talking to a fireman and a reporter from the evening news.

"This big guy heard the baby crying, and came right in and got us," she said through joyful tears. "He wrapped his shirt around the baby, and when the sirens came, he ran off down the street."

"Did you get his name?" the reporter asked.

"Yes, sort of," the woman replied. "He said it was Machiavelli."

That evening, the paper ran the story offering a reward to anyone with information about the identity of the Good Samaritan. No one came forward.[2]

COURAGE

MARTIN LUTHER KING JR.

Imagine that you have taken a stand, you have spoken words espousing your beliefs publicly, and then you are severely tested personally. Would you have the courage to stand up for what you said you believe, especially when the things you love most are threatened? In some cases, following through on your beliefs with consistency in your actions requires personal risk. It is said that until we are willing to die for the larger, greater thing, we have not truly begun to live.

Martin Luther King was in the process of leading a boycott against the segregated city bus system at a local church when he was informed that someone had firebombed his home. That information produced a feeling of intense concern because he believed that both his wife and his young child were in the house.

He rushed home, and from a distance he could see smoke coming from his house. In front of his home, a large group of civil rights followers were gathered. They described how a bomb had exploded on his front porch and the glass had been blown out of the lower section of the house. They gave him the good news that his wife and child had escaped safely.

Walking onto the destroyed porch, he turned and looked out on the crowd. They were rightfully enraged about what had happened to their leader. Many in the angry crowd had armed themselves with weapons and were calling for justice or revenge. As the local police arrived, a violent confrontation seemed inevitable. King sensed the potentially dangerous situation and raised his hand, quieting the crowd. His words and actions in this moment of crisis remained consistent with his beliefs. "My wife and baby are alright. I am asking that you put down your weapons and go home. We have the weapon of nonviolence, the breastplate of righteousness, the armor of truth. Remember what the Bible tells us: 'Do not be overcome by evil, but overcome evil with good.'"[1]

By having his beliefs and actions remain in alignment at this moment of truth, he continued the transformation of this nation. Coaches and athletes can help equip themselves to act appropriately in accordance with what they stand for by anticipating confrontational situations before they happen.

BRAVE THREE HUNDRED
ADAPTED BY JAMES BALDWIN

The famous battle at the narrow Pass of Thermopylae took place in 480 BC, when Xerxes led a Persian army into Greece. Even though they were defeated at Thermopylae, the Spartans' heroic stand against overwhelming odds inspired the Greeks in later resistance. The battle forever made Sparta's name synonymous with courage. All of Greece was in danger. A mighty army, led by Xerxes, the great king of Persia, had come from the east. It was marching along the seashore, and in a few days would be in Greece. Xerxes had sent messengers into every city and state, demanding that they send him water and earth as symbols that the land and the sea were his. The Greeks refused, and resolved to defend their freedom against the invaders. There was a great stir throughout all the land. The Greeks armed themselves and hurried to go out and drive back their foe. There was only one way by which the Persian army could go into Greece on that side, and that was through a narrow pass between the mountains and the sea. It was called the pass at Thermopylae, a word which meant "hot gates" because of the hot springs nearby.

The pass was guarded by Leonidas, the king of the Spartans, with only a few thousand troops. They were greatly outnumbered by the Persian army, but they felt confident. They had positioned themselves in the narrowest part of the pass, where a few men armed with long spears could hold back an entire company. The first Persian wave of attack started toward the pass at dawn. The Spartan scouts reported that there were so many troops their arrows would darken the sun like a cloud. "So much the better," Leonidas said. "We can fight better in the shade."

The arrows came down, but the Greeks' shields deflected them, and their long spears held back the Persians who pressed into the pass. The invaders attacked again and again, but each time they were repulsed with terrible losses. At last Xerxes sent forward his best troops, known as the Ten Thousand Immortals, but even they fared no better against the determined Greeks. After two days of attacks, Leonidas still held the pass.

That night a man was brought to Xerxes' camp. He was a Greek who knew the local terrain well, and he was ready to sell a secret: the pass was not the only way through. A hunters' footpath wound the long way around, to a trail along the spine of the mountain. It was held by only a handful of Greeks. They could be easily routed and then Xerxes could attack the Spartan army from the rear. The treacherous plan worked. The men guarding the secret trail were surprised and beaten. A few managed to escape in time to warn Leonidas. The Greeks knew that if they did not abandon the pass at once, they would be trapped. Leonidas also knew he must delay Xerxes longer while the Greek cities prepared their defenses. He made his decision. He ordered almost all of his troops to slip through the mountains and back to their cities—where they would be needed. He kept his royal guard of three hundred Spartans as well as a few other troops, and prepared to defend the pass to the end. Xerxes and his army came forward. The Spartans stood fast, but one by one they fell.

When their spears broke, they stood side by side, fighting with swords or daggers or only their fists. All day long they kept the Persian army at bay. When the sun went down, there was not one Spartan left alive. Where they had stood was only a heap of the slain warriors, all bristled over with spears and arrows. Xerxes had taken the pass, but at a cost of thousands of men and a delay of several days. The time cost him dearly. The Greek navy was able to gather its forces, and soon afterward, it managed to drive Xerxes back to Asia. Many years later a monument was erected at the pass of Thermopylae, inscribed in memory of the courageous stand of a few in defense of their homeland.[2]

HERNAN CORTES

In the 16th century, when given the task of invading a dangerous island with his troops, Spanish conquistador and leader, Hernan Cortes, was concerned about the commitment of some of his men. After departing the boats and arriving on land, Cortes immediately ordered the ships burned. By burning his own boats, he was sending a clear message to his army, "There is no turning back. We will either succeed here or die here." Excuses for not committing were gone. Burn the boats!"

JOHN CHALLIS

When John Challis, a devout sports fan for his eighteen years of life, found out he was going to die, he knew that he would have a whole new outlook on life. Two years before, a doctor told him that he had a ten-pound cancerous tumor in his stomach, which was about the size of a football. After eighteen months of dealing with cancer, John entered his senior year at Freedom High School in western Pennsylvania, and as part of having cancer, his outlook on fear took a drastic U-turn. Previously, John's fear of being hit by the pitch drove him from the sport that he loved, baseball. After being diagnosed, he thought of being hit by the ball, compared to cancer, as something ridiculous to be afraid of. He said, "Sports, that was my lov... still is but in a different way."

On April 11, 2008, John Challis took an opportunity to conquer his fear. His "different way" of playing baseball wasn't any different except for the flapjack that he wore to protect his ribs. Stepping up to that plate again helped him prove to himself that he could hit the ball and conquer his fear. In the fourth inning of the game at Freedom High School, John Challis was called up to pinch hit. As the ninety-three pound young man walked to the plate, he looked at the catcher's mask, which had the number eleven, John's number, written on it along with the initials J.C. John saw it, chuckled and said "nice mask." All he wanted was for people to pray for him. He didn't want anybody feel sorry for him. He hit the first pitch, a fastball thrown in the strike zone. He drilled it between first and second and it went into the outfield for a single. Halfway down the baseline he was yelling, "I did it! I did it!" He was one for one in his baseball career, batting 1.000 with one RBI.

Under his hat that day, John wrote the following: John Challis #11 Courage + Believe = Life. It became his motto and it also touched the lives of people he has never met all across the nation. His message lives on and will inspire many more in addition to the millions he has already touched. He taught his sister, Lexie Challis, to "live today's life, and live to the fullest today." It is through his quotes and messages like these that we will return to his story and look upon it again and again for advice while remembering the life of a very inspirational young man.

John Challis passed on Tuesday August 19, 2008, at his home in Pennsylvania.[3]

PAT TILLMAN

In 2001 Pat Tillman, aged twenty-seven, out of loyalty to the Cardinal football team, turned down a nine-million-dollar, five-year offer sheet from the Super Bowl champion St. Louis Rams. He also passed on a three-year, $3.6 million contract with the Arizona Cardinals to enlist in the Army in May 2002 in the wake of the September 11, 2001 terrorist attacks. Tillman was a member of the Second Battalion, 75th Ranger Regiment, based at Fort Lewis, Washington. The battalion was involved in Operation Mountain Storm in southeastern Afghanistan, part of the U.S. campaign against fighters of the al-Qaida terror network and the former Taliban government along the Afghanistan-Pakistan border. He was killed one night while serving his country.

Tillman had played four seasons with the Cardinals, winning league-wide respect as a smart and hard-hitting, if somewhat small and slow, defensive safety before he enlisted with his younger brother, Kevin Tillman. He set a Cardinals' record with 224 tackles in 2000 and warmed up for that year's training camp by competing in a 70.2-mile triathlon in June. Tillman, who at five-feet, eleven-inches tall and 200 pounds was considered undersized for his position. Nevertheless, he distinguished himself by his intelligence and appetite for rugged play. As a linebacker at Arizona State University, he was the Pacific Ten Conference's defensive player of the year in 1997. He graduated summa cum laude in 3.5 academic years as an academic All-American, earning a degree in marketing with 3.84 grade-point average. Pat Tillman is an example of a man who had everything going for him but was not satisfied with the fact that he had not done something special for his country. He wanted to be a hero for his country and not just sit back and let others have that honor. He thought of others and placed them before himself and his dream career as a pro-football player. He conquered the fears and the difficulties, served his fellow Americans and gave his life doing it. He was a man of courage and a hero.[4]

EMPATHY

THE STORY OF THE LITTLE MOUSE

A mouse looked through a crack in the wall to see the farmer and his wife opening a package. What food might it contain? He was aghast to discover that it was a mousetrap. Retreating to the farmyard the mouse proclaimed the warning, "There is a mouse trap in the house, a mouse trap in the house!"

The chicken clucked and scratched, raised her head and said, "Excuse me, Mr. Mouse, I can tell this is a grave concern to you, but it is of no consequence to me. I cannot be bothered by it."

The mouse turned to the pig and told him, "There is a mousetrap in the house, a mousetrap in the house!"

"I am so very sorry, Mr. Mouse," sympathized the pig, "but there is nothing I can do about it but pray. Be assured that you are in my prayers."

The mouse turned to the cow. She said, "You say, Mr. Mouse. A mousetrap? Like I am in grave danger... NOT!"

The mouse returned to the house, head down and dejected, to face the farmer's mousetrap alone.

That very night a sound was heard throughout the house, like the sound of a mousetrap catching its prey. The farmer's wife rushed to see what had been caught. In the darkness, she did not see that it was a venomous snake whose tail the trap had caught. The snake bit the farmer's wife. The farmer rushed her to the hospital. She returned home with a fever.

Now everyone knows you treat a fever with fresh chicken soup, so the farmer took his hatchet to the farmyard for the soup's main ingredient. His wife's sickness continued so that friends and neighbors came to sit with her around the clock. To feed them, the farmer butchered the pig. The farmer's wife did not get well, and a few days later she passed away.

So many people came for her funeral that the farmer had the cow slaughtered to provide meat for all of them to eat.

So the next time you hear that someone is facing a problem and think that it does not concern you, remember that when the least of us is threatened, we all may be at risk.

We are all one family!

A PUPPY

A boy went to the pet store to buy a puppy. Four of them were sitting together, priced at $200 each. Then there was one sitting alone in a corner. The boy asked if that was from the same litter, if it was for sale, and why it was sitting alone. The storeowner replied that it was from the same litter, it was a deformed one, and not for sale. The boy asked what the deformity was. The storeowner replied that the puppy was born without a hip socket and had a leg missing. The boy asked, "What will you do with this one?" The reply was that it would be put to sleep. The boy asked if he could play with that puppy. The storeowner said, "Sure." The boy picked the puppy up and the puppy licked him on the ear. Instantly the boy decided that was the puppy he wanted to buy.

The storeowner said, "That is not for sale!" The boy insisted. The storeowner agreed. The boy pulled out $200 from his pocket and ran to get $200 from his mother. As he reached the door, the storeowner shouted after him, "I don't understand why you would pay full money for this one when you could buy a good one for the same price." The boy didn't say a word. He just lifted his left trouser leg, and he was wearing a brace.

The pet store owner said, "I understand. Go ahead, take this one."

This is empathy.

WET PANTS

Come with me to a third grade classroom, where a nine-year-old kid is sitting at his desk. All of a sudden, there is a puddle between his feet, and the front of his pants is wet. He thinks his heart is going to stop because he cannot possibly imagine how this has happened. It's never happened before, and he knows that when the boys find out he will never hear the end of it. When the girls find out, they'll never speak to him again as long as he lives.

The boy believes his heart is going to stop. He puts his head down and prays this prayer: "Dear God, this is an emergency! I need help now! Five minutes from now I'm dead meat."

He looks up from his prayer and here comes the teacher with a look in her eyes that says he has been discovered.

As the teacher is walking toward him, a classmate named Susie is carrying a goldfish bowl filled with water. Susie trips in front of the teacher and inexplicably dumps the bowl of water in the boy's lap.

The boy pretends to be angry, but all the while is saying to himself, "Thank you, Lord! Thank you, Lord!"

Now all of a sudden, instead of being the object of ridicule, the boy is the object of sympathy. The teacher rushes him downstairs and gives him gym shorts to put on while his pants dry out. All the other children are on their hands and knees cleaning up around his desk. The sympathy is wonderful, but as life would have it, the ridicule that should have been his has been transferred to someone else—Susie.

She tries to help, but they tell her to get out. "You've done enough, you klutz!"

Finally, at the end of the day, as they are waiting for the bus, the boy walks over to Susie and whispers, "You did that on purpose, didn't you?"

Susie whispers back, "I wet my pants once too."

GENEROSITY

THE PRECIOUS STONE

There was once a wise woman traveling in the mountains who found a precious stone in a stream. The next day she met another traveler who was hungry and she opened her bag to share her food. The hungry traveler saw the precious stone and asked if she might give it to him. She did so without hesitation. The traveler left, rejoicing in his good fortune. He knew the stone was worth enough to give him security for a lifetime. However, a few days later he came back to return the stone to the woman who had given it to him.

"I've been thinking," he said. "I know how valuable the stone is, but I'm giving it back in the hope that you can give me something even more precious. I want you to give me what you have within you that enabled you to give me the stone."

RYAN HRELJAC

Six-year-old Ryan Hreljac listened intently to his teacher's lesson one day. What he heard was a story about a land and its people; people who were living their lives very differently from his own. They didn't have luxuries. They didn't even have clean water to drink. They would have to walk miles to get clean water. Ryan wanted to do something to help them. When Ryan got home from school that day, he asked his parents to give him money for the people his teacher had told him about. Ryan's parents told him that if he really felt that strongly about it, he could earn the money. Ryan took them up on their offer and raised $70 in four months doing chores for them and their neighbors. Ryan wasn't satisfied though. He wanted $2,000. That would be enough to build a well in this

African village. He was determined he was going to build a well, because that's what they needed. He put his next plan of action in place. He began speaking to members of area schools, clubs, and churches about his "dream well." He captured the attention of his community and a family friend, who decided to write about his quest in the local newspaper. It wasn't long before Ryan had the $2,000 for his well. What has happened since the day he learned about the lack of drinkable water in Africa has saved the lives of thousands of people around the world. After the first well, Ryan is reported to have said that the ripple effect took over and one goal began to lead to another. Ryan now has a foundation called the Ryan's Well Foundation, which continues to raise money to help people not only in Africa but also around the world. In 1998 Ryan had the desire to build a well for the people in Africa. By 2007, Ryan's Well Foundation had built 255 wells in twelve countries and had raised 1.5 million dollars. Ryan has also visited countries all around the world, some of which are: Africa, Australia, China, Germany, Italy, England, The Netherlands, Mexico, Scotland, Uganda, United States, and Japan.[1]

THE DRUM

A poor woman had only one son. She worked hard cleaning houses and grinding grain for the well-to-do families in town. They gave her some grain in return and she lived on it, but she could never afford to buy nice clothes or toys for her son. Once, when she was going to the market with some grain to sell, she asked her son, "What can I get you from the market?" He promptly replied, "A drum! Mother, get me a drum." The mother knew she would never have enough money to buy a drum for him. She went to the market, sold the grain, and bought some graham flour and some salt. She felt sad that she was coming home empty-handed. Then, she saw a nice piece of wood on the road. She picked it up and brought it home to her son. The son didn't know what to do with it, but he carried it with him when he went out to play.

An old woman was lighting her woodstove with some cow-dung patties. The fire was not catching. There was smoke all around and it made the old woman's eyes water. The boy stopped and asked why she was crying. She said that she couldn't light her fire and cook. The boy said, "I have a nice piece of wood and you can start your fire with it." The old woman was very pleased, lit the fire, made some bread, and gave a piece to the boy.

He took the bread and walked on until he came upon a potter's wife. Her child was crying and flailing his arms. The boy stopped and asked her why the child was crying. The potter's wife said the child was hungry and she had nothing in the house to give him. The boy gave the bread in his hand to the hungry child, who ate it eagerly and stopped crying. The potter's wife was grateful to the boy and gave him a pot.

When he walked on, he came to the river, where he saw a washer man and his wife quarreling. The boy stopped and asked the man why he was scolding and beating his wife. The washer man said, "This woman broke the only pot we had. Now I've nothing to boil my clothes in before I wash them." The boy said, "Here, don't quarrel, take this pot and use it." The washer man was very happy to get a large pot. He gave the boy a coat in return.

The boy walked on. He soon came to a bridge, where he saw a man shivering in the cold without so much as a shirt on him. He asked the man what had happened to his shirt, and the man said, "I was coming to the city on this horse. Robbers attacked me and took everything, even my shirt." The boy said, "Don't worry. You can have this coat."

The man took the coat and said, "You're very kind, and I want to give you this horse."

The boy took the horse, and very soon he ran into a wedding party with the musicians, the bridegroom, and his family all sitting under a tree with long faces. The boy stopped and asked why they looked so depressed. The bridegroom's father said, "We're all set to go in a wedding procession, but we need a horse for the bridegroom. The man who was supposed to bring it hasn't arrived. The bridegroom can't arrive on foot. It's getting late, and we'll miss the auspicious hour for the wedding."

The boy offered them his horse, and they were delighted. When the bridegroom asked him what he could do in return, the boy said, "You can give me something—that drum your musician is carrying." The bridegroom had no trouble persuading the drummer to give the drum to the boy. The drummer knew he could easily buy another with the money he was going to get.

The boy now rushed home to his mother, beating his new drum, and told her how he got it, beginning with a piece of wood from the roadside.

THE SAFE

Once upon a time, a greedy, rich man hired a great mathematician. The rich man wanted the mathematician to find the best way for him to make the greatest profit in everything he did. The rich man was building a huge safe, and his greatest dream was to fill it with gold and jewels.

The mathematician was shut away for months in his study, before finally believing he had found the solution. He soon found there were some errors in his calculations, so he started all over again.

One night he appeared at the rich man's house, with a big smile on his face: "I found it!" he said. "My calculations are perfect." The rich man was going on a long journey the next day and didn't have time to listen. He promised the mathematician he would pay him double his wages if he would take charge of the business while he was away and put the new formulas into practice. Excited by his new discovery, the mathematician was delighted to accept.

When the rich man returned, months later, he found all his possessions gone. Furious, he went to ask for an explanation from the mathematician. The mathematician calmly told him what he had done. He had given everything away to people. The rich man couldn't believe it, but the mathematician explained it further.

"For months I analyzed how a rich man could gain the maximum benefit, but what I could do was always limited. There's a limit to how much one man can do by himself. Then I understood the key was that many people could help us to achieve the aim. So the conclusion was that helping others was the best way to get more and more people to benefit us."

Disappointed and furious, the greedy man stormed off, desperate at having lost everything to the hare-brained schemes of a madman. However, while he was walking away disconsolately, several neighbors ran over, worried about him. All of them had been helped when the mathematician shared the rich man's fortune. They felt so grateful to him that they offered him the hospitality of their houses, and anything such a special man might need. The neighbors even argued over who would get to help him.

Over the next few days, he saw the full results of what the mathematician had calculated. Wherever he went, he was received with great honor, and everyone was willing to help him in whatever way possible. He realized that his not having anything had given him much, much more. In this way, he managed to quickly set up flourishing businesses, but this time he followed the brilliant mathematician's advice. No longer did he keep his riches in a safe or anything like it.

Instead, he shared his fortune among a hundred friends, whose hearts he had converted into the safest, most grateful, and fruitful of safes.

THE BOY AND THE ICE CREAM SHOP

One day, a ten-year-old boy went to an ice cream shop, sat at a table and asked the waitress, "How much is an ice cream cone?"

She replied, "Seventy-five cents." The boy started counting the coins he had in his hand. Then he asked how much a small cup of ice cream was. The waitress impatiently replied, "Sixty-five cents."

The boy said, "I will have the small ice cream cup." He ate his ice cream, paid the bill, and left. When the waitress came to pick up the empty plate, she was touched. Underneath were ten one-cent coins as a tip.

The little boy had consideration for the waitress before he ordered his ice cream. He showed sensitivity and caring. He thought of others before himself. If we all thought like the little boy, we would have a great place to live. Show consideration, courtesy, and politeness. Thoughtfulness shows a caring attitude.

WHERE DOES IT END?

There is a story about a wealthy farmer who was once offered all the land he could walk on in a day, provided he came back by sundown to the point where he started. To get a new start, early the next morning the farmer started covering ground quickly because he wanted to get as much land as he could. Even though he was tired, he kept going all afternoon because he didn't want to miss this once in a lifetime opportunity to gain more wealth.

Late in the afternoon he realized the condition he had to fulfill to get the land was to get back to the starting point by sundown. His greed had gotten him far enough. He started his return journey, keeping an eye on how close he was to sundown. The closer it got to sundown, the faster he ran. He was exhausted, out of breath, and he pushed himself beyond the point of endurance. He collapsed upon reaching the starting point and died. He did make it before sundown. He was buried and all the land he needed was a small plot.

HUMILITY

ABRAHAM LINCOLN

One of the finest examples of humility and relentlessness in the history of the United States is Abraham Lincoln. He suffered numerous defeats and disappointments over the course of thirty years, but he never quit striving for his goals. His goals were geared toward serving others in public office. An arrogant man would have quit, faced with so much failure and adversity.

1831 – He failed in business.

1832 – He finished eighth in a field of thirteen candidates for state legislature.

1833 – He again failed in business.

1835 – Lincoln was engaged to be married, but his sweetheart died.

1836 – He had a nervous breakdown and spent six months confined to his bed.

1838 – He was defeated for Speaker of the House.

1840 – He lost in his bid to become Elector.

1850 – A son died.

1855 – Lincoln ran for the Senate but was defeated.

1856 – He ran for Vice-President and lost.

1858 – He tried to get elected to the Senate again. He failed.

1860 – Lincoln was elected the 16th president of the United States.

Today he is considered one of the greatest leaders of all time.

THE GOLDEN SWANS

In a far-away kingdom, there was a river. This river was home to many golden swans. The swans spent most of their time on the banks of the river. Every six months, the swans would leave a golden feather as a fee for using the lake. The soldiers of the kingdom would collect the feathers and deposit them in the royal treasury.

One day, a homeless bird saw the river. "The water in this river seems so cool and soothing. I will make my home here," thought the bird.

As soon as the bird settled down near the river, the golden swans noticed her. They came shouting, "This river belongs to us. We pay a golden feather to the king to use this river. You cannot live here."

"I am homeless, brothers. I too will pay the rent. Please give me shelter," the bird pleaded. "How will you pay the rent? You do not have golden feathers," said the swans laughing. They further added, "Stop dreaming and leave at once." The humble bird pleaded many times, but the arrogant swans drove the bird away.

"I will teach them a lesson!" decided the humiliated bird.

She went to the king and said, "O, King! The swans in your river are impolite and unkind. I begged for shelter but they said that they had purchased the river with golden feathers."

The King was angry with the arrogant swans for having insulted the homeless bird. He ordered his soldiers to bring the arrogant swans to his court. In no time, all the golden swans arrived at the King's court.

"Do you think the royal treasury depends upon your golden feathers? You cannot decide who lives by the river. Leave the river at once or you all will be beheaded!" shouted the King.

The swans shivered with fear on hearing the King. They flew away never to return. The bird built her home near the river and lived there happily forever. The bird gave shelter to all other birds in the river.

HUMBLE CHICKEN

When Christian Herter was governor of Massachusetts, he was running hard for a second term in office. One day, after a busy morning chasing votes (and no lunch), he arrived at a church barbecue. It was late afternoon and Herter was famished. As Herter moved down the serving line, he held out his plate to the woman serving chicken. She put a piece on his plate and turned to the next person in line.

"Excuse me," Governor Herter said, "do you mind if I have another piece of chicken?"

"Sorry," the woman told him. "I'm supposed to give one piece of chicken to each person."

"But I'm starved," the governor said.

"Sorry," the woman said again. "Only one to a customer."

Governor Herter was a modest and unassuming man, but he decided that this time he would throw a little weight around. "Do you know who I am?" he said. "I am the governor of this state."

"Do you know who I am?" the woman said. "I'm the lady in charge of the chicken. Move along, mister."[1]

GHANDI LEADING WITH HUMILITY

One of the world's greatest leaders was also one of the most humble. Gandhi based his entire leadership on humility and a strong desire always to serve the neediest, downtrodden, and oppressed in the world. When Gandhi traveled, he was often offered the opportunity to be treated like royalty but always chose to be with the most common people. In that part of the world, that meant third class, described as being in close, extremely hot, crowded, filthy, uncomfortable quarters, often with farm animals. When Gandhi was invited to travel, he was usually met at his destination by the same wealthy and influential people of the country who had invited him to come.

When asked why he chose to travel in third class, his response was, "Because there is no fourth class." Traveling by steamship on one such trip to England, Gandhi chose the third-class section. Greeted by dignitaries as he stepped off the ship, he was dressed in a loincloth and leading a goat. He declined offers to stay in expensive hotels and instead stayed in the slums of London's east end. He met with the king of England, dressed as he was coming off the ship. Afterward, when asked by a reporter, "Is that what you wore when you met with the king?" Gandhi humbly responded, "Yes, the king wore enough clothes for both of us."

THE FOX AND THE CROW
AESOP

Vanity is largely a matter of self-control, or lack thereof. Others may try to feed our ego, but it is up to us to constrain it. A coal-black crow once stole a piece of meat. She flew to a tree and held the meat in her beak. A fox, who saw her, wanted the meat for himself, so he looked up into the tree and said, "How beautiful you are, my friend! Your feathers are fairer than the dove's. "Is your voice as sweet as your form is beautiful? If so you must be the queen of birds." The crow was so happy in his praise that she opened her mouth to show how she could sing. Down fell the piece of meat. The fox seized upon it and ran away.

THE OAK TREE AND THE REEDS

The oak tree always thought that he was far stronger than the reeds. He said to himself, "I stand upright in a storm. I don't bend my head in fear every time the wind blows. But these reeds are really so weak." That very night blew a storm and the mighty oak tree was uprooted. "Good God!" sighed the reeds, "our way is better. We bend but we don't break."
The moral of the story: "Pride hath a fall."

THE BEAR HUNT

Ben and Pete went out bear hunting. For four days they saw nothing. Each night they slept in a nearby village, bragging about how they were going to shoot a trophy bear and pledging part of the bear's skin against the cost of their hotel room and food. On the fifth day a huge bear appeared, and Ben said nervously to his friend, "I don't mind confessing that I'm afraid to take a shot at this bear." Pete laughed, "Just leave it to me." So Ben scrambled like lightning up the nearest tree, and Pete stood with his gun at the ready. The bear came lumbering on, and Pete began to grow more and more scared. At length he raised his gun to his shoulder, but by now he was trembling so much that, before he could take proper aim, his gun went off and missed the target. Pete, remembering that bears never touch a dead body, threw himself flat and held his breath. The bear came very close to Pete, sniffed all around him and finally took off. Ben, who had been watching the whole affair from his tree, now came down and, congratulating Pete on his amazing escape, asked him, "What did the bear whisper in your year?" Pete sheepishly replied, "Don't sell the bearskin before you catch the bear"
Talk is cheap.

INTEGRITY

A POUND OF BUTTER

There was a farmer who sold a pound of butter to the baker. One day the baker decided to weigh the butter to see if he was getting a pound. He found that he was not. This angered him and he took the farmer to court. The judge asked the farmer if he was using any measure. The farmer replied, "Your Honor, I am primitive. I don't have a proper measure, but I do have a scale." The judge asked, "Then how do you weigh the butter?" The farmer replied, "Your Honor, long before the baker started buying butter from me, I have been buying a pound loaf of bread from him. Every day when the baker brings the bread, I put it on the scale and give him the same weight in butter. If anyone is to be blamed, it is the baker."

What is the moral of the story? We get back in life what we give to others. Whenever you take an action, ask yourself this question: Am I giving fair value for the wages or money I hope to make? Honesty and dishonesty become a habit. Some people practice dishonesty and can lie with a straight face. Others lie so much that they don't even know what the truth is anymore. But who are they deceiving? Themselves.

CHARITY

THE GOOD SAMARITAN
RETOLD BY JESSE LYMAN HURLBUT

Jesus, who taught that we should love our neighbor as we love ourselves, told the parable of the Good Samaritan (Luke 10:29-37) in response to a question: "Who is my neighbor?" To understand the story fully, it is important to know that a "Good Samaritan" would have been a contradictory term for most Jews in Jesus' time because of a long-standing hostility between Jews and Samaritans. The traveler who comes to the wounded man's aid here is the least likely to show sympathy. Jesus gave the parable or story of "The Good Samaritan." He said, "A certain man was going down the lone road from Jerusalem to Jericho and he fell among robbers, who stripped him of all that he had, and beat him, and then went away, leaving him almost dead. It happened that a certain priest was going down that road, and when he saw the man lying there, he passed by on the other side. And a Levite also, when he came to the place, and saw the man, he, too, went by on the other side. But a certain Samaritan, as he was going down, came where this man was, and as soon as he saw him, he felt a pity for him. He came to the man and dressed his wounds, pouring oil and wine into them. Then he lifted him up and set him on his own beast of burden, and walked beside him to an inn. There he took care of him all night. And the next morning he took out from his purse two shillings, and gave them to the keeper of the inn, and said, 'Take care of him, and if you need to spend more than this, do so. When I come again I will pay it to you.' Which one of these three do you think showed himself a neighbor to the man who fell among the robbers?"

The scribe said, "The one who showed mercy on him."

Then Jesus said to him, "Go and do thou likewise."

By this parable Jesus showed that "our neighbor" is the one who needs the help that we can give him, whoever he may be.[1]

THE MIDAS TOUCH
JOHN DRYDEN

We all know the story of the greedy king named Midas. He had a lot of gold, and the more he had, the more he wanted. He stored the gold in his vaults and used to spend time every day counting it.

One day while he was counting a stranger came from nowhere and said he would grant him a wish. The king was delighted and said, "I would like everything I touch to turn to gold."

The stranger asked the king, "Are you sure?"

The king replied, "Yes."

The stranger said, "Starting tomorrow morning with the sun rays you will get the golden touch."

The king thought he must have been dreaming; this couldn't be true. The next day when he woke up, he touched the bed, his clothes—everything turned to gold. He looked out of the window and saw his daughter playing in the garden. He decided to give her a surprise and thought she would be happy. Before he went to the garden, he decided to read a book. The moment he touched it, it turned into gold and he couldn't read it. Then he sat to have breakfast and the moment he touched the fruit and the glass of water, they turned to gold. He was getting hungry and he said to himself, "I can't eat and drink gold." Just about that time his daughter came running and he hugged her and she turned into a gold statue. There were no more smiles left.

The king bowed his head and started crying. The stranger who gave the wish came again and asked the king if he was happy with his golden touch. The king said he was the most miserable man. The stranger asked, "What would you rather have, your food and loving daughter or lumps of gold and her golden statue?" The king cried and asked for forgiveness. He said, "I will give up all my gold. Please give me my daughter back because without her I have lost everything worth having."

The stranger said to the king, "You have become wiser than before," and he reversed the spell. King Midas got his daughter back in his arms, and he learned a lesson that he never forgot for the rest of his life.[2]

PATIENCE

THE JAPANESE JUDO MASTER

There was a young man who was in a horrible accident. It left him without his left arm. He was a valiant guy, though, and never let that stop him. He decided to take up judo. He began his lessons with an old Japanese judo master. He was a good coach, and the young man knew it. He decided he would do his best to always listen to his coach and try to do everything he asked of him. After three months he began to get frustrated because his coach had only taught him one move. He finally broke down one day and asked, "Coach, aren't there any more moves I can learn?" "That is the only move you need to know," was the answer he got. He didn't really understand, but he humbly kept training.

About a year later it was time for his tournament. The young man was amazed at how easily he won first two contests. The third one was a bit more challenging, but still he won when his opponent got impatient and charged imprudently. He used his one move yet again and won the match. This put him in the finals. Everyone was amazed: one arm, first tournament, and the finals. Everyone was amazed except his coach. The final match was kind of scary. His opponent was bigger, faster, stronger, and very experienced. The match got ugly quickly—so ugly that the ref called a time-out at one point. "Keep going, you are doing fine," his coach reassured him. "If he drops his guard, attack." As the contest continued, the young man patiently waited to see if his opponent would drop his guard even for a second. His opponent made that critical mistake. The young man used the only move he had learned and he pinned him. He won his very first tournament.

On the way home the young man just couldn't hold in his curiosity any longer. "Coach, how did I win with only one move?" His coach, not the least bit surprised that he won, answered him. "It's really quite simple. First, you have almost mastered one of the most difficult throws in all of judo. Second, the only known defense for that move is for your opponent to grab your left arm."

A NEW YORK TAXI DRIVER'S STORY
KENT NERBURN

I arrived at the address and honked the horn. After waiting a few minutes, I honked again. Since this was going to be my last ride of my shift I thought about just driving away, but instead I put the car in park and walked to the door and knocked. "Just a minute," answered a frail, elderly voice. I could hear something being dragged across the floor.

After a long pause, the door opened. A small woman in her 90s stood before me. She was wearing a print dress and a pillbox hat with a veil pinned on it, like somebody out of a 1940s movie. By her side was a small nylon suitcase. The apartment looked as if no one had lived in it for years. All the furniture was covered with sheets.

There were no clocks on the walls and no knickknacks or utensils on the counters. In the corner was a cardboard box filled with photos and glassware.

"Would you carry my bag out to the car?" she asked.

I took the suitcase to the cab, then returned to assist the woman.

She took my arm and we walked slowly toward the curb.

She kept thanking me for my kindness. "It's nothing," I told her. "I just try to treat my passengers the way I would want my mother to be treated."

"Oh, you're such a good boy," she said.

When we got in the cab, she gave me an address and then asked, "Could you drive through downtown?"

"It's not the shortest way," I answered quickly.

"Oh, I don't mind," she said. "I'm in no hurry. I'm on my way to a hospice."

I looked in the rear-view mirror. Her eyes were glistening. "I don't have any family left," she continued in a soft voice. "The doctor says I don't have very long." I quietly reached over and shut off the meter.

"What route would you like me to take?" I asked.

For the next two hours, we drove through the city. She showed me the building where she had once worked as an elevator operator. We drove through the neighborhood where she and her husband had lived when they were newlyweds. She had me pull up in front of a furniture warehouse that had once been a ballroom where she had gone dancing as a girl. Sometimes she'd ask me to slow in front of a particular building or corner and would sit staring into the darkness, saying nothing.

As the first hint of sun was creasing the horizon, she suddenly said, "I'm tired. Let's go now."

We drove in silence to the address she had given me. It was a low building, like a small convalescent home, with a driveway that passed under a portico.

Two orderlies came out to the cab as soon as we pulled up. They were solicitous and intent, watching her every move. They must have been expecting her.

I opened the trunk and took the small suitcase to the door. The woman was already seated in a wheelchair.

"How much do I owe you?" She asked, reaching into her purse.

"Nothing," I said.

"You have to make a living," she answered.

"There are other passengers," I responded.

Almost without thinking, I bent and gave her a hug. She held onto me tightly.

"You gave an old woman a little moment of joy," she said. "Thank you."

I squeezed her hand and then walked into the dim morning light. Behind me, a door shut. It was the sound of the closing of a life.

I didn't pick up any more passengers that shift. I drove aimlessly lost in thought. For the rest of that day, I could hardly talk. What if that woman had gotten an angry driver or one who was impatient to end his shift? What if I had refused to take the run or had honked once, then driven away? On a quick review, I don't think that I have done anything more important in my life. We're conditioned to think that our lives revolve around great moments. But great moments often catch us unaware, beautifully wrapped in what others may consider a small moment.[1]

THE TORTOISE AND THE HARE
AESOP

There once was a speedy hare who bragged about how fast he could run. Tired of hearing him boast, the slow and steady tortoise challenged him to a race. All the animals in the forest gathered to watch.

Hare ran down the road for a while and then paused to rest. He looked back at the slow and steady tortoise and cried out, "How do you expect to win this race when you are walking along at your slow, slow pace?"

Hare stretched himself out alongside the road and fell asleep, thinking, "There is plenty of time to relax."

Tortoise walked and walked. He never, ever stopped until he came to the finish line.

The animals who were watching cheered so loudly for Tortoise, they woke up Hare.

Hare stretched and yawned and began to run again, but it was too late. Tortoise was over the line.

After that, Hare always reminded himself, "Don't brag about your lightning pace, for slow and steady won the race!"

THE CARPENTER

An elderly carpenter was ready to retire. He told his employer/ contractor of his plans to leave the house-building business and live a more leisurely life with his wife, enjoying his extended family. He would miss the paycheck, but he needed to retire. They could get by.

The contractor was sorry to see his good worker go and asked if he could build just one more house as a personal favor. The carpenter said yes, but in time it was easy to see that his heart was not in his work. In a rush to get the house done, he was very impatient. He resorted to shoddy workmanship and used inferior materials. It was an unfortunate way to end his career.

When the carpenter finished his work in record time and the contractor came to inspect the house, the contractor handed the front door key to the carpenter. "This is your house," he said, "my gift to you for your retirement."

What a shock! What a shame! If he had only known he was building his own house, he would have done it all so differently. He would have taken his time and put much more care into his work. Now he had to live in the home he had built using shoddy workmanship.

So it is with us. We build our lives in a distracted way, reacting rather than acting, hurrying and scurrying along, willing to put up less than the best. At important points we do not give the job our best effort. Then, with a shock, we look at the situation we have created and find that we are now living in the house we built. If we had realized, we would have done it differently.

Think of yourself as the carpenter. Think about your house. Each day you hammer a nail, place a board, or erect a wall. You should build patiently and wisely. It is the only life you will ever build. Even if you live it for only one day more, that day deserves to be lived graciously and with dignity. Building your life is a lot like building a house. Take care...

Your life today is the result of your attitudes and choices in the past. Your life tomorrow will be the result of your attitude and your choices today.

TRUE PATIENCE

A little old couple walked into a fast food restaurant. The little old man walked up to the counter, ordered food, paid, and took the tray back to the table where the little old lady sat. On the tray was a hamburger, a small bag of fries and a drink. Carefully the old man cut the hamburger in two, and divided the fries into two neat piles. He sipped the drink and passed it to the little old lady, who took a sip and passed it back. A young man at a nearby table watched the old couple and felt sorry for them. He offered to buy them another meal, but the old man politely declined, saying that they were used to sharing everything. The old man began to eat his food, but his wife sat still, not eating. The young man continued to watch the couple. He still felt he should be offering to help. As the little old man finished eating, the old lady had still not started on her food. "Ma'am, why aren't you eating?" asked the young man sympathetically.

The old lady looked up and said politely, "I'm waiting for the teeth."

THANKFULNESS

A MOTHER'S LOVE

A little boy came up to his mother in the kitchen one evening while she was fixing supper and handed her a piece of paper that he had been writing on. After his mom dried her hands on an apron, she read it, and this is what it said:

- For cutting the grass: $5.00
- For cleaning up my room this week: $1.00
- For going to the store for you: $.50
- Babysitting my kid brother while you went shopping: $.25
- Taking out the garbage: $1.00
- For getting a good report card: $5.00
- For cleaning up and raking the yard: $2.00
- Total owed: $14.75

Well, his mother looked at him standing there, and the boy could see the memories flashing through her mind. She picked up the pen, turned over the paper he'd written on, and this is what she wrote:

- For the nine months I carried you while you were growing inside me: No Charge
- For all the nights that I've sat up with you, doctored, and prayed for you: No Charge
- For all the trying times, and all the tears you've caused through the years: No Charge
- For all the nights filled with dread, and for worries I knew were ahead: No Charge
- For the toys, food, clothes, and even wiping your nose: No Charge Son, when you add it up, the cost of my love is: No Charge.

When the boy finished reading what his mother had written, there were big tears in his eyes. He looked straight at his mother and said, "Mom, I sure do love you." Then he took the pen, and in great big letters he wrote "PAID IN FULL."

THE BLIND BOY

I was disillusioned by life with good reason to frown,
For the world was intent on dragging me down.
And if that weren't enough to ruin my day,
A young boy out of breath approached me, all tired from play.
He stood right before me with his head tilted down,
And said with great excitement, "Look what I found!"
In his hand was a flower; what a pitiful sight,
With its petals all worn—not enough rain, or too little light.
Wanting him to take his dead flower and go off to play,
I faked a small smile and then shifted away.
But instead of retreating he sat next to my side
And placed the flower to his nose and declared with surprise,
"It sure smells pretty and it's beautiful too.
That's why I picked it. Here, it's for you."
The weed before me was dying…or dead.
Not vibrant of colors, orange, yellow, or red.
But I knew I must take it, or he might never leave.
So I reached for the flower and replied, "Just what I need."
But instead of him placing the flower in my hand,
He held it mid-air without reason or plan.
It was then that I noticed for the very first time,
That weed-toting boy could not see: he was blind.
I heard my voice quiver, tears shone like the sun,
As I thanked him for picking the very best one.
"You're welcome," he smiled, and then ran off to play,
Unaware of the impact he'd had on my day.
I sat there and wondered how he managed to see
A self-pitying woman beneath an old willow tree.
How did he know of my self-indulged plight?

Perhaps from his heart he'd been blessed with true sight.
Through the eyes of a blind child, at last I could see
The problem was not with the world; the problem was me.
And for all of those times I myself had been blind,
I vowed to see the beauty in life, and appreciate every second
    that's mine.
And then I held that wilted flower up to my nose
And breathed in the fragrance of a beautiful Rose
And smiled as I watched that young boy, another weed in his hand
About to change the life of an unsuspecting old man.[1]

HOT CHOCOLATE

Some graduate students, who were well established in their careers, were talking at a reunion and decided to go visit their old retired university professor. During their visit, the conversation turned to complaints about stress in their work and lives. Offering his guests hot chocolate, the professor went into the kitchen and returned with a large pot of chocolate and an assortment of cups—porcelain, glass, crystal, some plain looking, some expensive, some exquisite—telling them to help themselves to the drink.

When they all had a cup of hot chocolate in hand, the professor said, "Notice that all the nice looking expensive cups were taken, leaving behind the plain and cheap ones. While it is normal for you to want only the best for yourselves, that is the source of your problems and stress. The cup that you're drinking from adds nothing to the quality of the hot chocolate. In most cases, it is just more expensive and, in some cases, even hides what we drink. What all of you really wanted was hot chocolate, not the cup; but you consciously went for the best cups…and then you began eyeing each other's cups.

"Now consider this: Life is the hot chocolate; your job, money, and position in society are the cups. They are just tools to hold and contain life. The cup you have does not define, nor change, the quality of life you have. Sometimes, by concentrating only on the cup, we fail to enjoy the hot chocolate God has provided us.

"God makes the hot chocolate, man chooses the cups. The happiest people don't have the best of everything. They just make the best of everything that they have. Live simply. Love generously. Care deeply. Speak kindly. And enjoy your hot chocolate!"

BAD PARROT – A THANKSGIVING STORY

A young man named John received a parrot as a gift. The parrot had a bad attitude and an even worse vocabulary.

Every word out of the bird's mouth was rude, obnoxious, and laced with profanity. John tried and tried to change the bird's attitude by consistently saying only polite words, playing soft music, and doing anything else he could think of to clean up the bird's vocabulary.

Finally, John was fed up, and he yelled at the parrot. The parrot yelled back. John shook the parrot, and the parrot got angrier and even ruder. John, in desperation, threw up his hand, grabbed the bird, and put him in the freezer. For a few minutes the parrot squawked and kicked and screamed. Then, suddenly, there was total quiet. Not a peep was heard for over a minute.

Fearing he'd hurt the parrot, John quickly opened the door to the freezer. The parrot calmly stepped out onto John's outstretched arms and said, "I believe I may have offended you with my rude language and actions. I'm sincerely remorseful for my inappropriate transgressions, and I fully intend to do everything I can to correct my rude and unforgivable behavior."

John was stunned at the change in the bird's attitude.

As he was about to ask the parrot what had made such a dramatic change in his behavior, the bird spoke-up, very softly, "Excuse me…may I ask what the turkey did?"

ACRES OF DIAMONDS

There was a farmer in Africa who was happy and content. He was happy because he was content. He was content because he was happy. One day a wise man came to him and told him about the glory of diamonds and the power that goes along with them. The wise man said, "If you had a diamond the size of your thumb, you could have your own city. If you had a diamond the size of your fist, you could probably own your own country." Then he went away.

That night the farmer couldn't sleep. He was unhappy and he was discontent. He was unhappy because he was discontent and discontent because he was unhappy. The next morning he arranged to sell his farm, took care of his family, and went in search of diamonds. He looked all over Africa and couldn't find any. He looked all through Europe and couldn't find any. When he got to Spain, he was emotionally, physically, and financially broke. He became so disheartened that he threw himself into the Barcelona River and committed suicide.

Back home, the person who had bought his farm was watering camels at a stream that ran through the farm. Across the stream, the rays of the morning sun hit a stone and made it sparkle like a rainbow. He thought it would look good on the mantelpiece. He picked up the stone and put it in the living room. That afternoon the wise man came and saw the stone sparkling. He asked, "Is Hafiz back?"

The new owner said, "No, why do you ask?"

The wise man said, "Because that is a diamond. I recognize one when I see one."

The man said, "No, that's just a stone I picked up from the stream. Come, I'll show you. There are many more." They went and picked some samples and sent them for analysis. Sure enough, the stones were diamonds. They found that the farm was indeed covered with acres and acres of diamonds.

What is the moral of this story? There are three:

1. When our attitude is right and we are thankful for what we have, we are more apt to realize that we could be walking on acres and acres of diamonds. Opportunity is always under our feet. We don't have to go anywhere. All we need to do is recognize it.

2. The grass on the other side always looks greener. Be thankful for what you have rather than always wanting that green grass on the other side of the fence.

3. While we desire the grass on the other side, there are others who desire the grass on our side. There are lots of people out there who are not as well off as you are and would be happy to trade places with you.

SACRIFICE

ARE YOU A CARROT OR A TEA BAG?

Take two boiling pots of water. Into one drop a carrot and then into the other drop a tea bag.

The carrot goes in straight and sturdy; it has been well raised. Over time, the heat and pressure of the boiling water causes the carrot to become soft and pliable. It will bend in any direction you choose to bend it. Or it just becomes mush.

The tea bag is totally different from the carrot. When it hits the water, it almost immediately changes the water. By adding heat and pressure, the tea bag changes the environment into something much better.

The boiling water represents the environment in which we are placed. Do we let the environment change us in a negative way? (Carrot.) Or do we change the environment around us in a positive way? (Tea bag.)

Which do you want to be? A carrot or a tea bag? Being a tea bag takes sacrifice. The tea bag must "give of itself" in order to change the water.

THE CHARGE OF THE LIGHT BRIGADE
ALFRED TENNYSON

Tennyson based this famous poem on the Battle of Balaklava, fought on October 25, 1854, during the Crimean War, in which a small force of British cavalry made a daring but disastrous assault against a Russian artillery line. After the attack, only 195 of the 673 men in the Light Brigade answered muster call. Some find it fashionable to ridicule this poem as a glorification of war to those who blindly and stupidly follow orders. The fact is that there are times when obedient acts of self-sacrifice and courage merit both admiration and profound gratitude.

Half a league, half a league,
Half a league onward,
All in the Valley of Death
Rode the six hundred.
"Forward, the Light Brigade!
Charge for the guns!" he said:
Into the Valley of Death
Rode the six hundred.
"Forward, the Light Brigade!"
Was there a man dismay'd?
Not tho' the soldier knew
Someone had blunder'd:
Theirs not to make reply,
Theirs not to reason why,
Theirs but to do and die:
Into the Valley of Death
Rode the six hundred.
Cannon to right of them,
Cannon to left of them,
Cannon in front of them
Volley'd and thunder'd;
Storm'd at with shot and shell,
Boldly they rode and well,
Into the jaws of Death,
Into the mouth of Hell
Rode the six hundred.[1]

MICHAEL MONSOOR
NORMAN FULKERSON

On September 29, 2006, Ramadi, Iraq, was considered the most dangerous city on planet earth for American servicemen. Michael Monsoor was there in the midst of it all. He was a member of the elite branch of the Navy called SEALS, which stands for Sea, Air and Land. On that day, he was on a rooftop over-watch in the most contested part of the city called the Ma'laab district. Positioned near the only exit, with an MK 48 machinegun in hand, he was providing security for two SEAL snipers who lay in prone positions on either side of him. Moments later a fragmentation grenade bounced off his chest and landed on the ground. As a heavy-weapons machine gunner, his position, while patrolling the streets of Ramadi with Delta Company, was right behind the point man. The responsibility for protecting the rest of the unit fell squarely on his shoulders. It was an appropriate position for a Catholic young man named after the warrior angel, Saint Michael. He was also a SEAL communicator, which required him to carry a rucksack full of communications equipment in addition to his MK 48 machine gun full of ammunition. He carried the extra 100 pounds, without complaint, in temperatures as high as 130 degrees.

In May of 2006, during his first month in Iraq, his unit came under fire during counter-terrorist operations. Heavy enemy automatic weapons fire resulted in a wounded SEAL left exposed to enemy fire. Michael threw caution to the wind and ran directly into the line of fire to help the injured soldier. As gunfire chewed up the asphalt around him, Michael snatched the wounded soldier from the jaws of death with one arm, returned enemy fire with the other and then dragged him to safety. He then maintained suppressive fire while the wounded SEAL received tactical casualty treatment. After loading his wounded teammate onto an evacuation vehicle, he returned to the battle. This act of heroism earned him a Silver Star and a reputation for putting others first. Such protection was sorely needed, especially considering that seventy-five percent of the missions involving Michael's platoon came under attack. Thirty-five escalated into heated firefights taking place in "streets that were paved with fire." During eleven of those missions Michael's leadership, guidance, and decisive action were key in saving the lives of many of his men. For his heroism he was awarded the Bronze Star. The story that accompanies the medal describes how he "exposed himself to heavy enemy fire while shielding his teammates with suppressive fire. He aggressively stabilized each chaotic situation with focused determination and uncanny tactical awareness. Each time the terrorists assaulted his team with small arms fire or rocket propelled grenades, he quickly assessed the situation, determined the best course of action to counter the enemy assaults, and implemented his plan to gain the best tactical advantage." As extraordinary as all of this is, it was merely a prelude to the defining moment of his life in the rooftop over-watch. When the grenade landed in front of him, Michael

Monsoor knew that the length of the fuse would not allow him to toss it out. He also knew that he was two short weeks away from returning home to family and friends. With the only exit door at his back, a live grenade at his feet and two Navy SEALs in front of him, he was faced with the hardest decision of his life. It was one of those rare moments when life passes before your eyes. Having already endured so many hardships and numerous brushes with death, no one would have faulted him had he chosen a path to safety.

"He chose a different path," said Mr. Winter, "a path of honor." On numerous occasions, Michael Monsoor stared death in the face in his heroic defense of others. Once again he and death would meet and once again he put others first. With unflinching selflessness he gave his life so that others might live. In so doing, he saved the lives of three Navy SEALs and eight Iraqi soldiers. One of the survivors described how "Mikey" looked death in the face that day and said, "You cannot take my brothers, I will go in their stead."

"He never took his eye off the grenade; his only movement was down and toward it," said a twenty-eight-year-old lieutenant who lived to tell the story. "He undoubtedly saved mine and the other SEALs' lives." Another eyewitness described Michael's countenance as "completely calm, showing no fear only resolve." It could easily be said of him what General Pericles said in his funeral oration about the warriors of ancient Athens: "He passed away from the scene, not of his fear, but of his glory." Michael Monsoor was immediately evacuated to a battalion aid station. Fr. Paul Anthony Halladay, his platoon chaplain, was with Michael as he passed away approximately thirty minutes later. It was an appropriate end for a soldier who, according to many reports, was a practicing Catholic. His fellow soldiers told how he frequently attended mass "with devotion" before his operations. Patricia Monsoor, his aunt, and godmother, said he "went to confession frequently," and "other soldiers who were not practicing would sometimes follow [him to Mass] because of his good example."

When he was posthumously awarded the Medal of Honor, a tearful President Bush reminded the audience that the day Michael Monsoor died was the feast of Saint Michael the Archangel. An emotional Donald Winter quoted a passage from Scripture already remembered by so many to describe Michael Monsoor. "Greater love than this no man hath, that a man lay down his life for his friends."

"When it came down to laying down his life for his friends, his faith allowed him to [do so] without a moment's hesitation," said Father Halladay.

The most moving tribute to Petty Officer Michael Monsoor was that given by Lt. Commander John Willink during an evening ceremony at the Navy Memorial honoring the fallen hero. He described in detail a photo of Michael (released shortly after his death). The picture shows Michael walking at the head of his platoon, through the war-torn streets of Ramadi. They are shrouded in a greenish yellow mist used to mask their movements from the enemy. In spite of the chaos and danger that surrounds them, Michael is calm, almost smiling. "As I look at this picture," Lt. Willink said, "I hear a voice in a humble but confident tone."

He then finishes his speech with the words he imagines Michael saying to him. They are words that I feel Michael Monsoor is saying to every American who appreciates the unbelievable sacrifice he made in a land far from his family and the country he loved.

"I am Michael Monsoor. I am patrolling the streets of Ramadi... My eyes sting from the sweat, my gun and gear are heavy, but these things do not bother me. There is no comfort here, but this is the life I have chosen, and there is no place I would rather be... I am ready.

"I am Michael Monsoor, I miss my family. I want to hold my nieces and nephews again. I want to make them smile and laugh, but I am far from home. Instead, I smile at the Iraqi children when we pass them by. When we encounter Iraqi families, I treat them with respect and dignity. I know the importance of family because there is nothing more important to me than my family.

"I am Michael Monsoor. I love my country, my fellow SEALs and the men fighting alongside us. I have lived life to its fullest. I have not looked back. I leave nothing but love, and I have no regrets.

"I am Michael Monsoor. I have given everything... for you!"[2]

THE MONKEYS AND THE CRABS
DAVID THOMSON

All the monkeys that live in the forests near the great sea in the south watch the tide running out, hoping to catch the sea-crabs that are in the soft earth. If they can find a crab above the ground, they immediately catch and eat it. Sometimes, the crabs bury themselves in the mud, and the monkeys, seeing the tunnels they have made, reach down into them with their long tails, and torment the crabs until they, in anger, seize the tormenting tail and are drawn out and devoured by their cunning foes. Sometimes, alas, the crab fails to come out! No matter with what strength the monkey pulls and tugs, the crabs do not appear, and the poor monkey is held fast, while the tide comes in and drowns it. When the tide goes out again, leaving the luckless monkey dead on the beach, the crabs come out from their strongholds and feast on their enemy.[3]

I KNEW YOU WOULD COME

There were two childhood buddies who went through school and college and even joined the army together. War broke out and they were fighting in the same unit. One night they were ambushed. Bullets were flying all over, and out of the darkness came a voice, "Harry, please come and help me." Harry immediately recognized the voice of his childhood buddy, Bill. He asked the captain if he could go. The captain said, "No, I can't let you go, I am already short-handed, and I cannot afford to lose one more person. Besides, the way Bill sounds, he is not going to make it." Harry kept quiet. Again the voice came, "Harry, please come and help me." Harry sat quietly because the captain had refused earlier. Again and again the voice came. Harry couldn't contain himself any longer and told the captain, "Captain, this is my childhood buddy. I have to go and help." The captain reluctantly let him go. Harry crawled through the darkness and dragged Bill back into the trench. Bill was dead. Now the captain got angry and shouted at Harry, "Didn't I tell you he was not going to make it? He is dead, you could have been killed, and I could have lost a hand. That was a mistake." Harry replied, "Captain, I did the right thing. When I reached Bill, he was still alive and his last words were 'Harry, I knew you would come.'"

WISDOM

THE FROGS AND THE WELL
AESOP

The prudent person looks before leaping. Two frogs lived together in a marsh. One hot summer the marsh dried up, and they left it to look for another place to live in, for frogs like damp places if they can get them. By and by they came to a deep well, and one of them looked down into it and said to the other, "This looks a nice cool place. Let us jump in and settle here." The other, who had a wiser head on his shoulders, replied, "Not so fast, my friend. Supposing this well dried up like the marsh, how should we get out again?" Think twice before you act.

THE WISE OLD MAN

Once there was an old man who lived in a tiny village. Although poor, he was envied by all, for he owned a beautiful white horse. Even the king coveted his treasure. A horse like this had never been seen before—such was its splendor, its majesty, its strength.

People offered fabulous prices for the steed, but the old man always refused. "This horse is not a horse to me," he would tell them. "It is a person. How could you sell a person? He is a friend, not a possession. How could you sell a friend?" The man was poor and the temptation was great. But he never sold the horse.

One morning he found that the horse was not in the stable. All the village came to see him. "You old fool," they scoffed, "we told you that someone would steal your horse. We warned you that you would be robbed. You are so poor. How could you ever hope to protect such a valuable animal? It would have been better to have sold him. You could have gotten whatever price you wanted. No amount would have been too high. Now the horse is gone, and you've been cursed with misfortune."

The old man responded, "Don't speak too quickly. Say only that the horse is not in the stable. That is all we know; the rest is judgment. If I've been cursed or not, how can you know? How can you judge?"

The people contested, "Don't make us out to be fools! We may not be philosophers, but great philosophy is not needed. The simple fact that your horse is gone is a curse."

The old man spoke again. "All I know is that the stable is empty, and the horse is gone. The rest I don't know. Whether it be a curse or a blessing, I can't say. All we can see is a fragment. Who can say what will come next?"

The people of the village laughed. They thought that the man was crazy. They had always thought he was a fool; if he wasn't, he would have sold the horse and lived off the money. But instead, he was a poor woodcutter, an old man still cutting firewood and dragging it out of the forest and selling it. He lived hand to mouth in the misery of poverty. Now he had proven that he was, indeed, a fool.

After fifteen days, the horse returned. He hadn't been stolen; he had run away into the forest. Not only had he returned, he had brought a dozen wild horses with him. Once again, the village people gathered around the woodcutter and spoke. "Old man, you were right and we were wrong. What we thought was a curse was a blessing. Please forgive us."

The man responded, "Once again, you go too far. Say only that the horse is back. State only that a dozen horses returned with him, but don't judge. How do you know if this is a blessing or not? You see only a fragment. Unless you know the whole story, how can you judge? You read only one page of a book. Can you judge the whole book? You read only one word of a phrase. Can you understand the entire phrase?

"Life is so vast, yet you judge all of life with one page or one word. All you have is a fragment! Don't say that this is a blessing. No one knows. I am content with what I know. I am not perturbed by what I don't."

"Maybe the old man is right," they said to one another. So they said little. Down deep, they knew he was wrong. They knew it was a blessing. Twelve wild horses had returned with one horse. With a little bit of work, the animals could be broken and trained and sold for much money.

The old man had a son, an only son. The young man began to break the wild horses. After a few days, he fell from one of the horses and broke both legs. Once again the villagers gathered around the old man and cast their judgments.

"You were right," they said. "You proved you were right. The dozen horses were not a blessing. They were a curse. Your only son has broken his legs, and now in your old age you have no one to help you. Now you are poorer than ever."

The old man spoke again. "You people are obsessed with judging. Don't go so far. Say only that my son broke his legs. Who knows if it is a blessing or a curse? No one knows. We only have a fragment. Life comes in fragments."

It so happened that a few weeks later the country engaged in war against a neighboring country. All the young men of the village were required to join the army. Only the son of the old man was excluded, because he was injured. Once again the people gathered around the old man, crying and screaming because their sons had been taken. There was little chance that they would return. The enemy was strong, and the war would be a losing struggle. They would never see their sons again.

"You were right, old man," they wept. "God knows you were right. This proves it. Your son's accident was a blessing. His legs may be broken, but at least he is with you. Our sons are gone forever."

The old man spoke again. "It is impossible to talk with you. You always draw conclusions. No one knows. Say only this: Your sons had to go to war, and mine did not. No one knows if it is a blessing or a curse. No one is wise enough to know. Only God knows."

SERVICE

COUNT THAT DAY LOST
GEORGE ELIOT

We can look back on each day as being either lost or spent. Mary Ann
Evans, better known as George Eliot (1819-1880), showed us how to tell
the difference, and what is worth a day's expense.

If you sit down at set of sun
And count the acts that you have done,
And, counting, find
One self-denying deed, one word
That eased the heart of him who heard,
One glance most kind
That fell like sunshine where it went—
Then you may count that day well spent.

But if, through all the livelong day,
You've cheered no heart, by yea or nay—
If, through it all
You've nothing done that you can trace
That brought the sunshine to one face—
No act most small
That helped some soul and nothing cost—
Then count that day as worse than lost.[1]

LIFE IN THE FAST LANE

A young and successful executive was traveling down a neighborhood street, going a bit too fast in his new Jaguar. He was watching for

kids darting out from between parked cars and slowed down when he thought he saw something.

As his car passed, no children appeared. Instead, a brick smashed into the Jag's side door! He slammed on the brakes and spun the Jag back to the spot from where the brick had been thrown.

He jumped out of the car, grabbed a kid and pushed him up against a parked car, shouting, "What was that all about and who do you think you are? Just what the heck are you doing?"

Building up a head of steam he went on. "That's a new car and the repairs are going to cost a lot of money! Why did you do it?"

"Please, mister, please. I'm sorry, I didn't know what else to do," pleaded the youngster. "I threw the brick because no one else would stop." Tears were dripping down the boy's chin as he pointed around the parked car.

"It's my brother," he said. "He rolled off the curb and fell out of his wheelchair and I can't lift him up." Sobbing, the boy asked the man, "Would you please help me get him back into his wheelchair? He's hurt and he's too heavy for me."

Moved beyond words, the driver tried to swallow the rapidly swelling lump in his throat. He lifted the young man back into the wheelchair, took out his handkerchief and wiped the scrapes and cuts, checking to see that everything was going to be okay.

"Thank you and may God bless you," the grateful child said to him. The man then watched the little boy push his brother down the sidewalk toward their home.

It was a long walk back to his Jaguar, a long, slow walk.

He never did repair the side door. He kept the dent to remind him not to go through life so fast that someone has to throw a brick at you to get your attention.

HOW WOULD YOU LIKE TO BE REMEMBERED?

About a hundred years ago, a man looked at the morning newspaper and, to his surprise and horror, read his name in the obituary column. The newspapers had reported the death of the wrong person by mistake. His first response was shock. Am I here or there? When he regained his composure, his second thought was to find out what people had said about him. The obituary read, "Dynamite King Dies." Also, "He was the merchant of death." This man was the inventor of dynamite. When he read the words "merchant of death," he asked himself, "Is this how I am going to be remembered?" He got in touch with his feelings and decided that this was not what he wanted. From that day on, he started working toward peace. His name was Alfred Nobel, and he is remembered today for the great Nobel Prize.

Just as Alfred Nobel got in touch with his feelings and redefined his values, we should step back and do the same. What is your legacy? How would you like to be remembered? Will you be spoken well of? Will you be remembered with love and respect? Will you be missed?

THINK OF OTHERS

A man died and St. Peter asked him if he would like to go to heaven or hell. The man asked if he could see both before deciding. St. Peter took him to hell first, and the man saw a big hall with a long table, lots of food on it, and music playing. He also saw rows of people with pale, sad faces. They looked starved and there was no laughter. He observed one more thing. Their hands were tied to four-foot forks and knives and they were trying to get the food from the center of the table to put into their mouths, but they couldn't. Then, he went to see heaven. There he saw a big hall with a long table, lots of food, and music playing. He noticed rows of people on both sides of the table with their hands tied to four-foot forks and knives also. He observed there was something different here. People were laughing and were well fed and healthy. He noticed that they were feeding one another across the table. The results were happiness, prosperity, enjoyment, and gratification because they were not thinking of themselves alone. The same is true of our lives.

GROWING GOOD CORN – RCHLECTER FARMS

Schlechter Farms in Brooks, Oregon, grows award-winning corn. Each year they enter their corn in the state fair, where it usually wins a blue ribbon.

A few years ago, a newspaper reporter from the *Statesman Journal* in Salem interviewed Schlecter Farms and learned something interesting about how they grow their corn. The reporter discovered that Schlechter Farms shares their seed corn with their neighbors.

"How can you afford to share your best seed corn with your neighbors when they are your direct competitors?" the reporter asked.

"Why sir," said Mr. Schlechter, "didn't you know? The wind picks up pollen from the ripening corn and swirls it from field to field. If my neighbors grow inferior corn, cross-pollination will steadily degrade the quality of my corn. If I am to grow good corn, I must help my neighbors grow good corn."[2]

Schlecter Farms is very much aware of the connectedness of life. Their corn cannot improve unless their neighbor's corn also improves.

So it is with our lives. Those who choose to live in peace must help their neighbors live in peace. Those who choose to live well must help others to live well, for the value of a life is measured by the lives it touches. Those who choose to be happy must help others to find happiness by sharing each other's suffering and encouraging each other, for the welfare of each is bound up with the welfare of all.

If we want to grow good corn, we must help students, parents, and co-workers grow good corn.

If we want to grow happiness, we must help students, parents, and co-workers grow happiness.

JOY

THE BLOSSOMING FIG TREE

Once there was a young fig tree with leaves happy green, surrounded by fig trees of leaves happy green. The garden where he lived was welcoming, enjoyed by many as a haven of beauty and rest for the soul. Paths were worn by the feet of friends, lovers, and even the solitary ones who came to hear nature, feel the earth, and breathe color. The fruit of the fig trees was delightful and sweet, its pulp desired by many, its nectar enjoyed by all who came to the garden. The time for blossoms had arrived and the fig tree felt the power of life surge through him, beginning at the roots, traveling through the trunk, making his limbs shiver. But alas, no blossoms came. He shook his limbs and tried again. *Surely, that was only a fluke,* he thought. The other youthful fig trees were blossoming around him. He searched deep within the core, wiggled his roots and concentrated on producing beauty. Nothing. Disheartened, the fig tree bowed his head and wept silently. *Maybe next year.* Time and time again, after dismal winter had passed, he would witness the life of spring as shrubs and plants, even stately trees would burst with flowers with such natural artistry that it would take even his breath away. He prayed that he too could add to the array of color and wonderment, hopeful that he could be fruitful so that others could enjoy the product of his love. One beautiful spring day, a visitor came to the garden and walked quietly among the flowers with a book under his arm and a blanket draped across his shoulder. He laid the blanket on the carpeted grass underneath the blossomless fig tree with leaves happy green. He read from his book, with a voice rich yet gentle. "Though the fig tree may not blossom... Yet I will rejoice and have joy in my Creator." The fig tree heard the words and in amazement came to the quiet realization that the power to blossom did not come from within him, but from He who had created him. With humble acceptance, he meditated on the words he just heard, happy to provide shade to his friend. His troubled heart finally at rest, the young fig tree thought, "In spite of my circumstance, I will have faith in my Creator, at peace with my lot, rejoicing and sharing what I do have with all who come underneath my happy green leaves."

JOY HEALING

Joy healing can come to you unsolicited, as an involuntary spiritual aid. Divine intervention is available to all of us. You may know what I mean. Have you ever been in the midst of an unsolvable crisis only to go to sleep, weary and care-worn? Hours later, you wake up relaxed and care-free. Then, perhaps without knowing why, you start your day energized as though all of life's disturbances have passed you by.

We are refreshed and quickly go on with our lives, almost forgetting the miracle of our crisis passing by. For instance, let's say a boss is making you miserable. You have visions of him or her firing you and putting you out of work at a time that the economy is very bad. You cannot resolve this. You go home and perhaps "dream out" the worst this situation could bring you. You may see yourself as being jobless and broke and living on the streets. Then, when the dream has been dreamt out, you wake and go to work only to find out that your boss has been transferred to a different part of the company, and even better than that, someone who likes and admires you is now your boss.

Joy is the divine spark that fuels our entire being. Joy is a means to an end and an end in itself.

THE JOY LIST

The most important gift you can give yourself is the Joy List. This list consists of everything and anything that brings you any amount of joy— the smell of fresh flowers, a child's smile, or finding money on the ground.

Begin your list with the most precious, the people in your life, and then move on to nature and the arts. Take this list out and reread it whenever you need to remind yourself of all the things you have that bring joy into your life. Appreciate.

When you find yourself all tense and overworked, take a five-minute break. Take a Joy Break. Pick something off your list to enjoy for just five minutes. Don't be so busy that you can no longer enjoy being! If you are so busy trying to be a success that you only have a short Joy List, remember that success is measured by the degree that you are enjoying peace. Sit down right now and write down ten things that make you joyful.

The Joy List can change your life. On this list goes everything that brings joy into your life. From sunshine to a stranger's smile—put anything that makes you smile, feel warm and fuzzy, or just plain happy on this list.

Examples of what can go on your list:

- Lazy Sunday afternoons
- The smell of fresh coffee
- The smell after a spring rain
- Warm sunshine
- Discount coupons
- Paid Holidays
- Playing with the grandkids
- Walks in the summer
- The smell of spaghetti sauce simmering
- Laughing
- Hugs
- Fireworks
- New babies

Begin your list, and add to it whenever you think of something that brings you joy. You now have a list that you can refer to at a moment's notice to remind yourself of all that you have to appreciate.

The wonderful thing about the Joy List is that you can fall back on it when the going gets tough. For example, your kids are having a slumber party and the constant giggling is going to drive you crazy (because it always does). Plan ahead and rent four classic comedy movies, and what do you know…you can make it through the night without stress!

MODERATION

THE ROMAN GAMES

The great battles of the Coliseum made famous in movies like *The Gladiator* began on a much smaller scale. The tradition started as a way to celebrate the funerals of important men. Two prisoners would fight to the death. Whoever killed his opponent first went free.

These battles grew in number and intensity as military officials and politicians competed to put on the grandest show. The contest also grew in popularity as the central source of entertainment for ordinary Romans. Sensing the people's fervent interest, in the year 40 BC Julius Caesar held the first games that were unconnected to a funeral.

The games quickly grew in size, scope, and barbarity. The Romans' appetite for the games was insatiable and eventually warranted building the famous Coliseum to hold the rabid fans. These fans constantly demanded a ratcheting up of the experience's intensity. In the same way that sleazy reality shows of today find new and degrading ways to bring in viewers, the gladiator games sought new twists to keep the audience interested. The games were meticulously planned to meet the spectators' expectations. What had started as a contest between gladiators became a bizarre and bloody circus where humans were fed to animals, animals were slaughtered for fun, and women, children, blind men, and dwarves were made to fight to the death.

Even brief pauses in the action bored the crowd, necessitating the building of elaborate tunnels facilitating the entrance and removal of warriors and animals with minimal interruption. People expected each show to be better and bloodier than the last. Yet the games ever-escalating intensity could not keep pace with the crowd's insatiable appetite for blood. It became impossible for Rome's rulers to keep up with the pace and costs of these elaborate spectacles, and the games eventually died out in the sixth century.

The story of the Roman games showcases a very important paradox: greater stimulation will not appease your desires; it will actually increase your appetite for them.

As we increase our stimulation, our appetite consequently rises to meet it. We then need even more stimulation to achieve the same pleasure the old level of stimulation gave us.

Yet the ratcheting up of stimulation will eventually reach the point of diminishing returns. As you seek higher and higher levels of stimulation, you eventually damage the delicate mechanisms your body and mind have for receiving and enjoying pleasure. We can overload our pleasure circuits and become numb to future enjoyments.

NOTES

Enthusiasm

1. Charles Schwab, "Guide to Finances." ://content.schwab.com/web/retail/public/book/. Accessed: November 2, 2012.

2. Arthur Motley, "Nothing happens until somebody sells something." http://www.barrypopik.com/index.php/new_york_city/entry/nothing_happens_until_somebody_sells_something.

Counsel

1. Charles Plumb: Insights Into Excellence, "Excerpt from Chapter 16, 'Packing Parachutes.'" http://speaker.charlieplumb.com/about-captain/parachute-story. Accessed: January 4, 2011.

Friendliness

1. Joseph Parry, "New and Old Friends." Public domain.

Gentleness

1. Richard Dunagin, "The Gold Fish." http://fullgospelassem.org/images/Word_Pro_-_KillerSoaps.pdfiss. Accessed: January 18, 2009.

Honor

1. Joseph Marshall, "The Lakota Indians." http://stephendpalmer.com/red-shirt-warrior-test/. Accessed: May 12, 2003.

Humor

1. Norman Cousins, "The Man Who Laughed In The Face of Death." http://margoparrowsmith.hubpages.com/hub/normancousins. Accessed: March 3, 2004.

Obedience

1. Archibald Rutledge, "Rocky Little Dog." http://deersearch.org/kevin-amstrong-article/. Accessed: February 15, 2003.

Servitude

1. Leo Tolstoy, Elias. Public domain.

2. This story originally appeared in the play "Some Folks Feel the Rain." http://blog.simpletruths.com/day-14-learn-from-old-warwick.

Initiative

1. Ken Keyes, Jr. http://worldprayerfoundation.com/resources/Ken%20 Keyes-Handbook%20to%20Higher%20Consciousness.pdf. Accessed: August 12, 2009.

Kindness

1. John Schlatter, "A Simple Act of Kindness." http://www.csc.villanova. edu/~jkearns/chicken.htmlI. Accessed: May 4, 2009.

Leadership

1. Jack Canfield, "The Golden Buddha." https://close2bliss.wordpress. com/2011/03/30/the-story-of-the-golden-buddha/. Accessed: September 28, 2009.

2. Angeles Arrien, "We Can Learn A Lot From Geese." http://www. brefigroup.co.uk/resources/view_product.do?product=11&category_ sname=freeIs. Accessed: December 7, 2011.

Loyalty

1. Rod Serling, "An Old Man and His Dog." http://www.aarf.org/Memorials/ NoDogsInHeaven.htm. Accessed: July23, 2008.

Respect

1. "Most Important Lesson." http://www.parablesite.com/.

Suffering a Cause

1. James Belasco, *Teaching Elephants to Dance* (Plume, 1990), p. 237.

2. Rev. Dr. Anthony Harvey, http://www.westminster-abbey.org/. Accessed: 2008.

Faithfulness

1. Triwik Kurniasari, "The true story of the faithful dog Hachiko." http://m. thejakartapost.com/news/2010/04/04/%E2%80%98hachiko-a-dog%E2%80%99s-story%E2%80%99-the-touching-true-story-a-sweet-loyal-dog.html. Accessed: March 4, 2010.

Tenacity

1. Florence Chadwick, "The True Story of Florence Chadwick." http:// mjeighty-two-waiting.blogspot.com/2010/01/true-story-of-florence-chadwick.html. Accessed: June 12, 2008.

2. Ernest Schackleton, South Pole.com. http://www.south-pole.com/ p0000097.htm: Accessed: May 29, 2010.

3. Charles Schulz, "Peanuts and Schulz." http://www.nytimes.com/ 2007/10/14/books/review/McGrath-t.html?pagewanted=all&_r. Accessed: December 28, 2010.

4. Harland Sanders, "Colonel Sanders' Cookbook and Autobiography." http://colonelsanders.com/bio.asp. Accessed February 12, 2013.

Understanding

1. John Godfrey Sax, "The Six Blind Men and the Elephant." http://www.constitution.org/col/blind_men.htm. Accessed August 11, 2012.

Poise

1. "A Smile" poem, Anonymous.

Fortitude

1. David Livingston, David Livingston Biography: http://www.biographyonline.net/adventurers/david-livingstone.html. Accessed: June 2, 2008.

Temperance

1. James Baldwin, "Ghengis Kahn and His Hawk." http://www.biography.com/people/genghis-khan-9308634 Accessed: March 14, 2008.

Hope

1. Roger William Thomas, "Keep Your Fork, the Best is Yet to Come." http://keepyourfork.net/keep-your-fork-inspirational-story. Accessed January 19, 2011.

Love

1. Dr. Joseph Brennermann, http://www.ynhh.org/physician-finder/detail.aspx?recid=4664. Accessed November 14, 2009.

2. Nancy Bouchard, http://www.ynhh.org/physician-finder/detail.aspx?recid=4664. Accessed October 12, 2010.

Courage

1. Martin Luther King, http://www.brainyquote.com/quotes/authorsm/martin_luther_king_jr.html. Accessed June 3, 2008.

2. James Baldwin, https://www.google.com/?gws_rd=ssl#q=james+baldwain. Accessed: September 22, 2012.

3. John Challis, https://www.google.com/?gws_rd=ssl#q=John+Challis. Accessed January 13, 2011.

4. Pat Tillman, https://www.google.com/?gws_rd=ssl#q=Pat+Tillman. Accessed June 11, 2012.

Generosity

1. Ryan Hreljac, http://myhero.com/hero.asp?hero=RYAN_HRELJAC. Accessed April 22, 2009.

Humility

1. Christian Herter, https://www.google.com/?gws_rd=ssl#q=Christian+Herter+. Accessed November 1, 2010.

Charity

1. Jesse Lymman, *The Book of Virtues for Young People: A Treasury of Great Moral Stories*, p. 87.
2. John Dryden, https://www.google.com/?gws_rd=ssl#q=JOHN+DRYDEN+. Accessed October 29, 2009.

Patience

1. Kent Nerburn, "The Cab Ride I'll Never Forget." http://zenmoments.org/the-cab-ride-ill-never-forget/. Accessed September 29, 2011.

Thankfulness

1. The Blind Boy. https://www.google.com/?gws_rd=ssl#q=a+new+yor+taxi+drivers+story. Accessed February 17, 2011.

Sacrifice

1. Alfred Tennyson, "The Charge of The Light Brigade."
2. Norm Fulkerson, http://www.ssptv.com/author-norman-fulkerson/. Accessed June 22, 2000.
3. Dave Tomson, http://www.davethomson.org/. Accessed December 29, 2014.

Service

1. George Eliot, "Count That Day Lost." Public domain.
2. The newspaper reporter in this story is myself, Randy Traeger.